Arbitration: A Very Short Introduction

Very Short Introductions available now:

Thomas Schultz and Thomas Grant

ARBITRATION

A Very Short Introduction

OXFORD
UNIVERSITY PRESS

OXFORD
UNIVERSITY PRESS

Great Clarendon Street, Oxford, OX2 6DP,
United Kingdom

Oxford University Press is a department of the University of Oxford.
It furthers the University's objective of excellence in research, scholarship,
and education by publishing worldwide. Oxford is a registered trade mark of
Oxford University Press in the UK and in certain other countries

First edition published in 2021

Impression: 1

Published in the United States of America by Oxford University Press
198 Madison Avenue, New York, NY 10016, United States of America

British Library Cataloguing in Publication Data

Data available

Library of Congress Control Number: 2020946014

ISBN 978-0-19-873874-9

Printed in Great Britain by
Ashford Colour Press Ltd, Gosport, Hampshire

Contents

Contents

Preface

Arbitration is a procedure for resolving disputes. It performs the functions of a court system but under private contract or other agreement. Like judges, arbitrators preside over compulsory proceedings resulting in legal decisions that are binding and enforceable. However, unlike judges, arbitrators are called upon to preside over such proceedings only when, and to the extent that, particular parties have agreed for them to do so. Parties—which might be individuals, corporations, and even countries—agree to arbitration when they need skilled individuals to settle a present or future dispute and, for one reason or another, they do not wish to go to court.

Though arbitration is in its essence a system of privatized justice, some disputes that parties bring to arbitration hold considerable interest for the public at large. To give an example from the 2000s, investors used arbitration to challenge the Russian Federation's nationalization of Yukos, a company that at its peak produced some 2 per cent of the world's oil. The sheer size of the assets at stake attracted widespread attention. In other arbitrations, the disputes directly implicate international relations. For example, India and Bangladesh used arbitration in the 2010s to delimit their disputed maritime boundary in the Bay of Bengal. Elsewhere, over the past several decades especially, arbitrations have pitted the sovereign rights of countries against the rights of investors protected under treaties. International investment arbitrations sometimes affect public policy of the countries involved in profound ways, as well as raising questions about the security of foreign investment. Arbitrators also hear cases on a more human scale. For example, doping allegations against athletes may go to arbitration, such cases being another example where arbitration from time to time enters the wider field of public view.

But arbitration also addresses disputes that are relatively prosaic. Disputes arising out of the sale of goods and services by companies to other companies, or indeed to individuals, account for a large number of arbitrations. Millions of routine transactions between individual consumers and companies, such as the purchase of an airline ticket, are carried out under contracts in which an arbitration clause can be buried. Few consumers understand the practical impact that an arbitration clause has on their rights. The prolific growth of arbitration has created a parallel system of justice, but how that system works and what it means for individuals subject to it for a long time remained almost unknown outside a small community of specialists.

With arbitration now widespread yet still not well understood, controversies have started to brew. Arbitration can make it difficult or impossible for a country to restructure its foreign debt during a time of financial crisis. It may compel an athlete to withdraw from competition without recourse to a court. A customer may be surprised to learn that her claim against a company will not proceed in court: the claim goes, instead, to arbitration—under procedures and rules that favour the company. Or so critics say when arguing against arbitration.

Proponents of arbitration, however, say that some of the characteristics of arbitration singled out by critics in truth make the case *for* it. Consumer disputes, say proponents of arbitration, need efficient settlement, not lengthy court proceedings that run up exorbitant lawyers' fees. Elite competitors know the rules—including the rules that make arbitration binding and final—and so it is with little justification that they protest over doping bans. Courts in some countries, say the proponents, are unreliable or corrupt, so getting out of the court system is prudent. The critics say that arbitration sacrifices transparency, public accountability, predictability, fairness, and access to justice.

Though arbitration typically takes place behind closed doors at locations of the parties' choosing such as hotels and office buildings, the proceedings may unfold much as they would in court. Sometimes parties, when choosing to arbitrate, opt for rapid, streamlined procedures. But not always. In arbitration, parties, represented by lawyers, make claims and counter-claims, allege facts, examine witnesses, submit legal arguments, rebut one another's allegations and submissions, and so on. How complex the procedure and how long it should take are matters that, like the decision whether to arbitrate in the first place, are in the hands of the parties.

Arbitration holds interest for the legal profession, because it furnishes a variety of procedural choices distinct from national court systems and thus has created new branches of law practice, with the commercial and professional opportunities that such growth creates. Yet many lawyers' understanding of arbitration remains rudimentary. For example, even lawyers who are highly accomplished, but who are not arbitration experts, sometimes confuse arbitration with mediation and conciliation. These are also alternatives to court, but are not compulsory procedures that produce binding and enforceable results. The decision that arbitrators hand down is no mere recommendation. It is a legal instrument that the parties are obliged to respect no less than a court judgment.

The aim of this book is to provide the reader with a lively and accessible account of the essentials needed to understand this system for settling disputes, where it comes from, how it works, and why it matters.

Chapter 1 relates the origins of arbitration. Chapter 2 explains how arbitration works in practice. Chapter 3 describes some of the main types of cases in which parties use arbitration. Chapter 4 explores how this method of dispute settlement relates to public courts, the law, and legal systems. Chapter 5 turns to the most politically charged type of arbitration, arbitration between an investor and a foreign government. Chapter 6 reflects on the future directions that arbitration might take.

List of illustrations

Chapter 1
What is arbitration and where does it come from?

Though one of the most salient features of arbitration today is that it removes a dispute from the court system, arbitration traces its origins to a time when courts barely existed. A reference to arbitration appears on a tablet recording the laws of the Old Assyrian Empire at the end of the 3rd millennium BCE—that is, around the time when glass was being invented and several centuries before the Great Pyramid of Giza was built. Julius Caesar in his *Commentaries on the Gallic War* described arbitration in ancient Ireland. There was arbitration in pre-Islamic Arabia, and the Old Testament refers to it. Arbitration also was known in societies in which institutions were well-established that a present-day observer would recognize as courts. References to it are recorded from Imperial China, Ancient India, Greece, and Rome and in the Quran. In late-medieval and early-modern Europe, arbitrators offered their services at trade fairs where travelling merchants turned to them for neutral dispute settlement, a service they did not trust local courts to provide. During the French Revolution in 1789, radicals sought to abolish courts; they saw arbitration as a panacea to cure the ills of an antiquated justice system.

Arbitration thus initially developed in the absence of courts and later in opposition to courts, or at least as an alternative to them. A theme—the sometimes fraught relation between arbitration and courts—can be discerned through much of the long history of arbitration and is very much visible today. However, to understand arbitration in its current variations we need to turn to relatively recent events, because it is there that the modern contours of arbitration have emerged.

The rise of modern arbitration

Three episodes illustrate the emergence of arbitration as we know it today. The first takes us to naval warfare in the 19th century; the second to Europe struggling to recover from the devastation of World War I; and the third to a failed arbitration in the 1950s that was entangled in the geopolitics of the Cold War and Middle East oil and that gave impetus to a new system for settling international investment disputes.

The first episode to which we turn is the Alabama Claims Arbitration, perhaps the most famous of all arbitration cases and that which legal historians identify as the starting point of the modern era of arbitration. The background to the case was the American Civil War and commerce raiding on the high seas. Ironically, the turbulent career of the Confederate naval cruiser *CSS Alabama* was most vividly depicted by Édouard Manet, a French impressionist known for his canvases of serene café life. Entitled *The Battle of the Kearsarge and the Alabama*, Manet's painting depicts the sinking of the *Alabama* in waters near Normandy by the United States (US) warship *USS Kearsarge* (see Figure 1). The year was 1864, and a battle of the American Civil War was unfolding in plain view of spectators on a French beach. The Confederate States had hoped the *Alabama* would save their rebellion from the strangling grip of the Union naval blockade. It did not. But it instigated a turning point in the history of arbitration, and, through arbitration, world politics to this day.

The international dispute over the *CSS Alabama* erupted not so much over what the ship did but over where, how, and for whom it

1. Édouard Manet, *The Battle of the Kearsarge and the Alabama.*

had been built. It had been built in Britain in secret for the navy of the rebel Confederate States of America. As the US government after the war would quite plausibly claim, this was a violation of Britain's avowed neutrality. A powerful ship the *Alabama* was, seizing scores of merchant vessels and leaving a trail of destruction from the coasts of New England in the US to the Cape of Good Hope in South Africa. In short, it had caused serious damage to the US, and the US wanted reparation. But wars for millennia had brought destruction; seldom, if ever, had a country's role in a war been the subject of a legal procedure.

3

The US and Great Britain tried to settle the matter through diplomacy. (At one point, the US demanded the cession of Canada.) The negotiations dragged on with no settlement in view. American business interests, however, pressed Washington. They wanted an outcome, soon, and with a cash award for their losses, which had been caused by acts that they saw as no better than piracy. After some hesitation came the historic breakthrough: the two governments resolved, by treaty, to establish an arbitration tribunal. The tribunal was to have five arbitrators. The US and Great Britain were each to name an arbitrator, and the king of Italy, the president of the Swiss Confederation, and the emperor of Brazil were each to name one of the remaining three. The tribunal was to meet in Geneva, a neutral ground.

Defying sceptics who doubted that two great powers would settle such a serious difference through a legal procedure, the arbitration went forward much as the treaty envisaged. The Alabama Claims Arbitration concluded on 14 September 1872. The Tribunal awarded the US an indemnity of US $15,500,000 in gold (roughly 5 per cent of the budget of Great Britain, or the modern equivalent of around US $20 billion). Great Britain paid it in full. The peaceful resolution of a major international dispute through a binding dispute settlement procedure marked a departure from centuries of *realpolitik* and earned the case justified renown. The room in Geneva's city hall in which the arbitration took place is still known as 'The Alabama Room'. With the signal success of the Alabama Claims Arbitration, the world in 1872 came to think of arbitration as a tool for the peaceful settlement of differences between nations.

Yet arbitration in modern times has grown most significantly in regard to commercial matters, not post-war settlement of international disputes. Nevertheless, to understand where arbitration as a tool for commercial dispute settlement comes from, it is again to the aftermath of a war that one turns. The second episode of the modern growth of arbitration starts in 1919.

It was a grey year in Europe. Four empires were in ruins. Civil wars were raging. And across the Continent's fringes, there was starvation, strife, and what today would be called ethnic cleansing and genocide. As for the nominal victors in the so-called Great War that had just ended, exhaustion and doubt overshadowed any sense of triumph. Fragile governments and febrile politics augured more suffering and crisis.

States had brought Europe to this nadir, and, so, thoughtful observers began to question whether, instead of turning to those same states, Europe might better look to private citizens to lead the way ahead. The new strain of thought entertained that, rather than by the diktat of kings and princes, or presidents and commissars, it would be by the initiative of private citizens that Europe might revitalize commerce and build the foundations for a lasting peace. The state had failed; it was time to organize the economy and society, and in a sense the law, without the state.

This is the idea that motivated the Merchants of Peace, a small group of industrialists, financiers, and traders who convened in Paris in 1919. At their meeting, the Merchants of Peace created a new organization—the International Chamber of Commerce. Non-governmental, non-profit, and constituted by members from many countries, the Chamber—or ICC—broke new ground. The purpose of the ICC, in the eyes of its founders in those dark days after World War I, was to regulate international commerce; and by regulating commerce to increase commerce; and by increasing commerce to make war so unprofitable that peace would become a permanent state of affairs. The ICC's constitution says that its 'fundamental objective' is to 'further the development of an open world economy with the firm conviction that international commercial exchanges are conducive to both greater global prosperity and peace among nations'.

To posit that commerce might be conducive to peace was not novel; people had put forward that proposition during the boom years before the recession of 1913 that had presaged the Great War. The novelty was in the creative work of the industrialists, financiers, and traders who now were giving the idea an independent, institutional foundation on which to grow. The ICC created rules and standards, common references for traders, financiers, and investors. Assisted by such outputs from the ICC, economic actors would know what to expect from those with whom they transacted, regardless of what country they came from, or in what country they did business. Greater reliability, predictability, and legal certainty would promote commerce, regardless of whether the rules and standards came from states or from a private initiative. States had shown themselves unable to cooperate toward such ends, and so the founders of the ICC took the initiative.

Rules such as those that the ICC created might look good on paper, but people would be insufficiently inclined to pay attention to them if they had no guardian to interpret and apply them in disputes. So in 1923 the ICC established the ICC International Court of Arbitration. Not a court in the sense of a public body with permanent judges, this new component of the ICC, instead, was a framework for commercial arbitration. In short order, it came to be the world's leading institution for commercial arbitration.

And so it remains to this day. Its prominence in the field of arbitration is such that, in the arbitration community, the ICC's Court is inseparably associated with the ICC itself. When arbitration lawyers refer to 'the ICC', they usually mean the institution and procedures for arbitration that the ICC created and, over time, refined and adapted to changing needs. The goal of ICC arbitration was, and remains, to allow businesspeople to settle their disputes as amicably, quickly, and inexpensively as possible. And then get back to business. Since its start, ICC arbitration has handled over 25,000 cases. The ICC is today, as it describes itself, 'a world business organization', boasting forty-five million companies in over a hundred countries. Its yearly arbitration case load continues to rise, and it serves businesses from every sector of the economy.

In addition to its success in its own right, the ICC was proof of the concept: over time, many further institutions have been established on a similar model. And, so, while remaining the preeminent commercial arbitration institution, the ICC today is one institution in a mosaic of institutions, rules, and practice. The Merchants of Peace and their private initiative in 1919 provided the seed for a vast ecosystem of commercial arbitration that now spans the globe.

Distinct from commercial disputes between business people or companies, and distinct from disputes between sovereigns such as the Alabama case, disputes sometimes arise between private investors and the governments of countries where they have invested. The third episode in the emergence of arbitration that we will consider concerned such a dispute. It is known to historians as the Abadan Crisis and to lawyers as the Anglo-Iranian Oil Company case of 1951–2. The case went to court, but the court had no jurisdiction to hear it. There was an arbitration clause, but the investor's best efforts to bring the case to arbitration were stymied. In its disastrous after-effects, the case demonstrated that the type of arbitration that the investor had sought—international investment arbitration—needed a stronger, more resilient framework if it were to succeed.

The case arose in the early 1950s against the backdrop of Cold War competition and political awakenings across the post-colonial world. Two decades earlier, in 1933, the Imperial Iranian government had granted the Anglo-Iranian Oil Company a concession for the exploitation of Iran's oil. The Company was a private enterprise, though the British government held a large part of its stock and it had British nationality. Over the years, Anglo-Iranian developed, at the city of Abadan in Iran, what grew into the world's largest oil operation: roads, hospitals, schools for

2. The Anglo-Iranian Oil Refinery at Abadan, Iran.

the company's employees, three ports, 450 oil wells, and an enormous oil refinery (see Figure 2). These constituted the largest overseas asset of any British company.

In April 1951, Mohammad Mosaddegh became prime minister of Iran. A charismatic politician and adroit parliamentarian, Mosaddegh had run on a platform that Iranian oil belonged to the Iranian people. He echoed the sentiment of many Iranians that the 120 million pounds sterling paid by the British company each year in exchange for the oil produced in Iran was a sordid pay-off and mere breadcrumbs, a relic of a time when European empires ruled colonies and dictated terms to weaker states such as Persia (as Iran was formerly known). Iran deserved more, Mosaddegh argued, and certainly needed more if it were to modernize and democratize. The Company at one point had proposed increasing Iran's share of the profits to 50 per cent, but Iran's parliament had rejected the proposal. In May 1951, Mosaddegh declared the Company nationalized.

Across the Atlantic, the nationalization of Anglo-Iranian triggered alarm. If Mosaddegh got away with it, a dangerous precedent would be set, and American investments in the region might well be the next target. Moreover, there was the matter of Iran's Communists: they were nominal allies of Mosaddegh, even if minor ones, but their mere presence provoked fear in Washington that the prime minister might join Iran to the Soviet bloc. In the end, Mosaddegh did not join the Soviet bloc, but nationalization of American assets in Iran ensued, and other countries in years to come similarly seized hold of Western investments.

The Anglo-Iranian Oil Company sought to defend its interests under the 1933 concession agreement. It was clear from the outset that this would be a difficult task. Taking the matter to an Iranian court would have been no use; no institution in Iran, even the shah, was prepared to water down, much less reverse, the nationalization decree. Courts in the United Kingdom (UK) and the US offered scarcely more hope: governments, protected by sovereign immunity, were (and are) notoriously difficult to sue in courts abroad. The principle known to lawyers as 'the act of state doctrine' would have stood in the way of British courts judging the legality of the nationalization decrees, even if they had found a way around sovereign immunity. And even if the Company were to have won a judgment in a Western court, there would have been nowhere to turn to collect on it against the Iranian state.

So the Company invoked an arbitration procedure. The arbitration procedure was contained in the 1933 concession agreement. The Company duly appointed Lord Radcliffe, an eminent British jurist, as its arbitrator. Iran, however, replied that '[t]he nationalization of the oil industry which is an act of sovereignty of the Iranian nation is not referable to arbitration, and no international institution is competent to examine this case'. Iran took no step to appoint its arbitrator. The British government was outraged, as was the British public. The government responded, shortly after, by bringing a case against Iran at the International Court of Justice (the ICJ or 'World Court') in The Hague requesting the ICJ to order Iran to submit to arbitration.

The ICJ, the UN's principal court, has jurisdiction only in matters between countries, and so the British government brought the case in the name of the UK, not the oil company. That gave rise to a fatal problem for the UK's case. The requirement that parties before the ICJ be countries is not the only limitation on that court's jurisdiction. For that court to have jurisdiction over any given country as defendant in a case, the country must consent to jurisdiction in regard to the suit brought by the claimant-country. Iran had not consented to jurisdiction in regard to the suit brought by the UK. The UK's lawyers tried valiantly to cast the 1933 concession agreement as an agreement between Iran *and Great Britain*, but the ICJ judged otherwise. The ICJ judged that this was an agreement between Iran and a private company (as the agreement plainly stated) and thus said nothing about Iran consenting to ICJ jurisdiction in regard to a suit by the UK. The UK's attempt to breathe life into an arbitration via the ICJ was to no avail. The arbitration did not go forward.

In a less anxious geopolitical climate, the matter would probably have ended there. The Anglo-Iranian Oil Company's stakeholders would have licked their wounds, perhaps levelling recriminations against the company managers under whom things had reached such an impasse. But the Cold War was at its height, and Western strategists feared that events in Iran had opened the door to Soviet expansion. British members of parliament, even as the UK was bringing its case before the ICJ, were asking His Majesty's government whether they were in touch with the US government about a military intervention. President Harry Truman was reluctant to get involved. Prime Minister Clement Attlee, whose approach was relatively cautious, nevertheless instituted an embargo against Iranian oil exports. Both leaders were soon replaced. With Winston Churchill back in 10 Downing Street and Dwight Eisenhower in the White House, the transatlantic posture hardened.

In August 1953, an operation by UK and US intelligence agencies overthrew Mosaddegh. The shah, who had fled after an earlier coup attempt had been botched, returned to Iran. The British Petroleum Company (BP), as Anglo-Iranian renamed itself in 1954, now conceded some of its share of the proceeds from Iran's oil to members of a consortium whose members were Western companies. Iran's share was set at 50 per cent—better than before, but the same percentage that Iran had earlier rejected. Under the post-coup arrangement Iran still had no right to audit the accounts.

The most significant impact of the Anglo-Iranian dispute was on Iran's future relations with the West. The Western investors had obtained favourable terms under the restored shah, but the seeds had been planted for distrust and a revolution which, when it came, would radically alter the face of global politics for decades to come. The failed Anglo-Iranian arbitration thus had consequences extending far beyond even the largest commercial dispute. It also had consequences for the future of international investment arbitration.

Well before the Islamic Revolution of 1979 made clear the full ramifications of the Anglo-Iranian affair, international lawyers recognized that their institutions had met with an egregious failure. Had not the 1933 concession agreement contained an arbitration clause? Had not the parties—Iran and the Company—bargained on this ancient method of dispute settlement resolving difficulties

11

that might arise in their relationship? Reading the concession agreement, a lawyer might well have answered in the affirmative. The problem was that agreements do not exist in a vacuum. They have to withstand the political turbulence of the time if they are to function as intended. A lesson learned from the failure of the Anglo-Iranian arbitration was this: a more robust legal arrangement was needed to support investor–state arbitration if investors such as Anglo-Iranian were to rely in the future on arbitration to address claims against a state. Within a decade, governments embarked on a new initiative for the purpose of creating just such an arrangement.

The initiative commenced in 1960, when the secretary-general of the United Nations (UN), Dag Hammarskjöld, proposed that states think about a treaty to support the arbitration of disputes between investors and foreign governments. The International Bank for Reconstruction and Development, an inter-governmental institution that the Allied Powers had set up at the end of World War II to help rebuild Europe, and better known as the World Bank, went to work to draft such a treaty. After lengthy investigation and consultation, the World Bank in 1965 had a final treaty text in hand. Entitled Convention on the Settlement of Investment Disputes between States and Nationals of Other States, the treaty received an enthusiastic response. Within a year, twenty states signed the Convention, and in 1966 it entered into force. Five years later, it had sixty-three signatory states. Today it has 163—more than three-quarters of the world's countries.

As Secretary-General Hammarskjöld had had in mind, the Convention gives support to arbitration of disputes between investors and foreign governments. Under the Convention, an investor proceeds before an international arbitral tribunal specifically chosen for the case. The Convention provides for international enforcement: it allows the investor who wins its case to demand payment in most types of government property wherever the property is located (so long as it is on the territory of a member state). Moreover, the Convention makes clear that offers by states to arbitrate disputes with foreign investors are not mere private matters that a state might dismiss under the prerogatives of a sovereign, the way Iran dismissed Anglo-Iranian's plea to respect the arbitration clause in the 1933 concession agreement: the Convention identifies the commitment to arbitrate as an international obligation, violation of which is to be likened to a violation of a treaty between states.

To administer arbitrations that investors bring under its terms, the Convention also set up an institution: the International Centre for Settlement of Investment Disputes, or ICSID (see Figure 3). The Convention is in fact usually referred to by the name of that institution—thus the ICSID Convention. As measured by the number of cases handled and their financial and political impact,

3.   Hearing in an ICSID Investment Arbitration, Washington, DC, November 2014.

ICSID is by far the most successful institution for arbitration of disputes between private investors and states. One may speculate how many crises of the kind that arose out of the Anglo-Iranian dispute ICSID has helped prevent. What is clear is that ICSID has supplied the more robust legal arrangement to support investor–state arbitration that was lacking in the 1950s. States, by participating in this arrangement, signal that commitments they make to foreign private investors to arbitrate disputes under ICSID are serious legal commitments and that they will be respected. ICSID has expanded the scope of arbitration for investment disputes to a degree comparable to that achieved by the ICC for commercial disputes.

So, since the mid-19th century, three major arbitration systems have emerged that function on the international level: one, between states, illustrated by the Alabama arbitration; the second, between businesses, epitomized in the ICC; and, the third, between investors and governments, which was given legal resilience in ICSID.

Arbitration also has expanded to cover disputes between businesses and consumers. Arbitration rules and institutions exist around the world to handle such disputes, but the phenomenon is most prevalent in the US. A small business with relatively few customers might propose arbitration to a customer, but arbitration of disputes between businesses and customers is especially associated with large businesses that have very large numbers of customers. Businesses with such numbers of customers did not always exist. This type of arbitration—consumer arbitration—thus is closely related to the emergence in the 20th century of the mass market economy and of companies that function on a national or international scale. Consumer arbitration, though its antecedents are less conspicuous than world wars and cold wars, nonetheless may be traced to modern developments in the world at large.

Arbitration's core

While arbitration takes many forms, all its forms share a core set of characteristics. Arbitration is a procedure in which certain parties choose a decision-maker and grant the decision-maker the exclusive power to render a decision on a dispute between them—usually referred to as an award—following a procedure that complies with some standard of fairness also agreed by the parties. By definition, the award issued in arbitration is legally binding upon the parties. It is directly enforceable against their assets.

Arbitration is based on an agreement between the parties. Without an agreement to arbitrate, there can be no arbitration. It is through their agreement that the parties grant a decision-maker—an arbitrator or a panel of arbitrators—the power to arbitrate. They may grant that power in regard to a dispute that has already arisen between them; or in regard to a category of disputes that might arise between them during the future course of their relationship. The award issued in arbitration is final; parties who enter an agreement to arbitrate waive rights that they might have had to take one another to court. It is a further core feature of arbitration that once two parties have lawfully agreed to arbitrate, and one of them properly lodges a claim against the other, arbitration is no longer a choice for the other party: it is a legal obligation. This is why jurists refer to arbitration as a *compulsory* dispute settlement procedure.

Though compulsory once chosen, arbitration is often idealized as a method of dispute settlement based upon freedom of choice. A central idea behind all arbitration is the freedom of the parties to choose a person (or people) to decide a dispute that has arisen between them (or a category of disputes that might arise between them during the future course of their relationship). Especially where the parties' business involves some specialist field that few judges understand, arbitration is attractive for this freedom it affords: it lets parties identify a decision-maker who understands their business. The parties may choose technical experts who have no formal legal background. When parties choose such non-lawyers, it is usually because the case turns on highly technical details peculiar to a specific sector. For example, a case concerning arcane financial instruments might be appropriate for an economist with expertise in financial services; a case concerning sophisticated machine tools, for a mechanical engineer. That said, it is most often lawyers who serve as arbitrators. The tendency of parties to choose lawyers as their arbitrators is not because of any formal requirements. To serve as an arbitrator, one need not be a lawyer, have a law degree, or hold a diploma in arbitration. Again, freedom to choose is a theme that runs through arbitration.

ICSID, which deals solely with investment arbitrations, does stipulate three requirements that an individual is to meet in order to serve as an arbitrator in ICSID proceedings: the person must be of high moral character; have recognized competence in the fields of law, commerce, industry, or finance; and can be relied upon to exercise independent judgment. No one, however, to our knowledge has ever been declared unfit to serve on grounds that they did not satisfy one or more of these ICSID requirements. Several arbitration institutions require that an arbitrator does not hold the same nationality as either of the parties to the arbitration. Some require proficiency in a given language. Where arbitration rules stipulate a nationality or language requirement, by contrast to the requirements for ICSID arbitrators just mentioned, this is in fairly definite terms, and parties insist on its observance. The parties themselves can further specify qualifications required of the arbitrators in an arbitration agreement. Arbitration lawyers will counsel against drafting highly exclusionary qualifications into the arbitration agreement: if the agreement overspecifies who is eligible to serve as an arbitrator, then there is a risk that such a person will not be found when needed, and the arbitration clause thus may become inoperable.

Notwithstanding the lack of formal qualifications for arbitrators in most arbitration proceedings, arbitrators are typically lawyers who specialize in arbitration. They tend to be partners or 'of counsel' in law firms. Some are solo practitioners, such as barristers in English chambers. A dwindling few are academics. An arbitrator ought to have a diary flexible enough to accommodate parties who will wish to fix dates on as expeditious a timeline as possible for the proceedings to reach a final award; this may be harder than it sounds, because the best arbitrators usually are the busiest. The arbitrator also must be free of conflicts of interest, a seemingly straightforward requirement but in practice sometimes controversial. An arbitrator typically has good management skills and business acumen. Proficiency in at least one of the main branches of arbitration is usually expected.

A judge serving on a national court might have a better grasp of law overall than the parties' chosen arbitrator. But the parties are not always concerned with the law overall; they may be focused on achieving a quick, pragmatic settlement. A dispute can get bogged down in legal technicalities, and so arbitration was long marketed precisely as a means to avoid overlawyering. At least in the early days of arbitration, a sense of lightness, simplicity, and business sense were its main appeals against the heavy bureaucratic and legal grind of the law courts. A commonsense decision-maker would clear through it all and render a quick and workable solution.

Yet disputes most often are not clear-cut. Arbitration, which long presented itself in opposition to courts, is at heart a legal mechanism. The arbitrators and the representatives arguing on behalf of the parties usually are all lawyers. And lawyers make themselves valuable, and expensive, by arguing the legal technicalities—which, in turn, entrenches the need for lawyers in arbitration. In the standard account of arbitration, good arbitrators kept the technicalities at bay. Arbitration today seldom comes very close to that account. Arbitration in recent decades has become a great deal more complex. It is no longer necessarily simpler, cheaper, or faster than litigation in court. A proceeding can end up heavily lawyerized, even though the parties opted out of court and elected instead to arbitrate.

What arbitration is not

Having now said what arbitration *is*, we should say a few words about what arbitration is *not*.

A common misunderstanding is that arbitration is just another form of negotiated settlement. It is not. The agreement to arbitrate is negotiated; but once in place the agreement is enforceable and, if properly invoked by one party, it sets in motion a compulsory procedure with the purpose of delivering a binding result.

Arbitration is not mediation. A mediator is a neutral party; to that extent the mediator might resemble an arbitrator. But a mediator's task is only to assist the parties in reaching an agreement themselves. If the parties fail to work out a consensual settlement, the mediation produces no binding outcome. The mediator might make suggestions. She might tell the disputants what is likely to happen if the mediation fails and they end up in court. A good mediator will give the parties a realistic picture of the strengths and weaknesses of their respective positions and also the costs and pitfalls of failing to reach a friendly resolution. But the parties are free to ignore a mediator. Even where one of the parties thinks that the mediator's suggested solution is perfect and begs the other party to accept it, the other party is free to reject it. In short, a mediator has no power to decide the case, no power to impose a result on the parties.

By contrast, when parties submit their dispute to arbitration, it is not open to either party to walk away. They have conferred a real power on the arbitrator. The arbitrator, like a judge, applies law (or, sometimes, other rules or principles) to facts in order to pronounce a decision, and that decision is binding. It is not a mere suggestion. The parties are not at liberty to ignore it. In this way, arbitration, like going to court, is adjudicative. The task of an arbitrator is to render a binding decision.

Arbitration is not a halfway house or a placeholder between negotiations and binding settlement: an arbitral award is final. Once an arbitral award has been properly delivered, a court will not re-hear the case. Procedures do exist in most national legal systems under which the loser in an arbitration can seek to have a court annul the decision of the arbitral tribunal. But the grounds for annulment of an arbitral award are much narrower than the grounds typically available for a court to overturn a court judgment. Some arbitration institutions, such as the ones mentioned in this chapter, have mechanisms to exercise basic quality controls over arbitral awards; but the controls are minimalist. Arbitration does not have an appeals procedure equivalent to that found in national court systems.

Some arbitration tribunals are international; some courts are international; but international arbitration tribunals are not international courts. This point should not be obscured by the fact that the word 'court' is found in the names of some of the institutional arrangements that have been created to support arbitration—for example the ICC's Court of Arbitration. The main examples of true courts performing international judicial functions today are the ICJ (the court that declined to order Iran to arbitrate the Anglo-Iranian Oil Company's claim), the International Tribunal for the Law of the Sea (ITLOS), and the World Trade Organization (WTO) Appellate Body. A common trait of these organs is that they are permanent. They exist under treaties—the ICJ under the UN Charter and its own Statute;

ITLOS under the UN Convention on the Law of the Sea (UNCLOS); the Appellate Body under the Agreement Establishing the WTO. They have permanent cadres of full-time professional judges. They hear all the disputes brought to them and over which their treaties give them jurisdiction, and they carry out their functions on a continuing basis. An arbitral tribunal, by contrast, is called into being by particular parties to settle a particular dispute. When a tribunal has given its final award to those parties in that dispute, the tribunal is finished. It disappears. The arbitrator or arbitrators who composed it go back to whatever they were doing (usually practising law). Even though some major arbitration systems, such as the ICC and ICSID, have standing organizations to support arbitrations, the arbitration tribunals that convene under those systems are transitory, like all arbitration tribunals.

Arbitration—usually—is not a mechanism for resolving disputes on the basis of general principles, such as fairness or equity, instead of law. Yet it is possible for the parties to specifically empower the arbitrator to do just that: that is, to decide the case on the basis of overall fairness independent of what the rules say. This remains a rare exception.

Arbitration is not a solution for every dispute that might arise in the world. Vast numbers of parties with vast numbers of disputes and potential future disputes are not subject to arbitration. One factor that limits the disputes that arbitration might settle is whether an agreement to arbitrate exists and, if so, what disputes the agreement covers. Another factor is that some disputes, even if the parties have said that they wish to settle them by arbitration, are not *arbitrable*. In particular, national law in many countries sets limits upon what disputes parties may agree to arbitrate.

Within a given relationship between two parties who have agreed to arbitration, there is often a mixture of issues: not all of the issues are legal; not all of the legal issues are within the scope of the parties' agreement to arbitrate; and not all of the legal issues that the parties would like to arbitrate are arbitrable. A challenge for arbitrators, and for the lawyers who represent the parties, is to isolate issues that are proper to arbitrate, if there are any, from those that are not. Arbitration is not an omnibus; it is not equipped to carry every type of issue to resolution.

Nor, however, does the mixing of different types of issues in a case necessarily preclude arbitration. For example, in a recent series of arbitrations under a bilateral investment treaty (BIT) between Ukraine and Russia, questions concerning Russia's geopolitical ambitions and aggression existed side by side with disputes over the seizure of private assets in Crimea. The former were treated as beyond the scope of arbitration; the latter, within it. An analogy may be seen in disputes between companies. Discrete issues subject to arbitration—such as allegations of patent or trademark infringement—might well be arbitrated; but competitors such as Apple and Google or Coca Cola and Pepsi are not likely to empower arbitrators to settle every issue that divides them.

An arbitrator is not to be equated to an elder diplomat whose good offices are called upon to oversee hostile parties negotiating a peace treaty. But, even as arbitrators can only do so much, isolating discrete legal issues and settling *those* issues can ameliorate the parties' antagonism. Winnowing down the issues that divide the parties, arbitration gives them a better chance at finding a general solution to their difficulties. As a mechanism that gets particular disputes out of the way, arbitration can make a negotiation more likely to succeed, whether between countries or in a business setting.

Sometimes, an arbitrator discovers that the parties are getting close to an amicable settlement and, thus, that the need for adversary proceedings is fading. Adroit arbitrators are careful not to overstep their bounds and start acting like mediators, which they are not; but they do not carry on oblivious to an opening that the parties themselves have arrived at. Where the parties' passions have cooled, and they are nearing a meeting of minds that would conclude their dispute but are hesitating at the final step, a confident arbitrator may supply a gentle prod or hint. Arbitration is not to fan the embers of a dispute that has obviously passed its most heated stage.

Interestingly, evidence suggests that arbitrators are more likely to encourage settlement if judges in their home culture are required by law to promote settlements in court. Though they are not obliged to conduct the arbitral procedure by the rules of any given court system, arbitrators appear to imitate the judges with whom they are most familiar.

So we have seen what arbitration is, what it is not, where it came from, and what it seeks to achieve. The task for Chapter 2 is to show how arbitration works in practice: what steps parties must take for an arbitration to go forward, how they choose their arbitrators, how arbitrators conduct an arbitration proceeding, and what happens after the arbitrators have issued their award.

Chapter 2
How arbitration works

Arbitration works differently in important respects from litigation in court. Arbitration takes place if and only if parties have consented to it. Their consent needs to make clear how, specifically, arbitration is going to work for them. It can do this by referring to some existing set of rules or an institution that can answer that question; it can also contain a bespoke set of rules crafted specially for those parties.

By consenting to arbitration, the parties have taken their dispute out of court. An arbitral award is final and without appeal. Under most arbitration agreements, once the arbitrator or arbitral tribunal has given the final award, arbitral jurisdiction comes to an end, and so there is no place for a party to turn to appeal against an adverse award. However, a losing party in arbitration nevertheless may have opportunities to challenge an award, including in proceedings in national courts.

Though arbitration is a private institution and, thus, not directly attached to the executive apparatus of the state that courts may rely on to enforce their judgments, parties in some situations may use courts, and through them the executive apparatus to assist in arbitral proceedings. A national court might, in principle, get involved in practically any stage of an arbitral proceeding, though, again, the specifics of how varies depending on the specifics of the arbitration.

The UN's International Law Commission (the ILC) in 1949 chose arbitral procedure as one of its first topics of priority for possible codification. The ILC's function is to study selected international law topics and, if appropriate, to set out proposed texts that states might adopt as treaties, or that states, courts, arbitral tribunals, and other parties might use as guides to the law. The ILC's proposal for a treaty on arbitral procedure met strong headwinds in the General Assembly of the UN. So the Commission set aside that idea and opted instead, in 1958, to adopt *Model Rules on Arbitral Procedure*. But even this text has had very little influence. General international law principles, such as good faith and the rules of treaty interpretation, apply in an arbitration when called for. Other than that, rules of universal application are lacking that specify how arbitration works. Party consent and party choice remain the central concepts behind arbitration. A profusion of arbitral arrangements has arisen.

Most or all arbitrations, however, have certain features in common.

Agreeing to arbitration

The first step to arbitration is to consent to it. Parties may consent to arbitration in any number of ways. In commercial relations, a typical approach is to include an arbitration clause in a contract. Such a clause will typically be in the later or final sections of the contract. Where the contract contains no arbitration clause, the parties still are free to conclude an arbitration agreement: they may do so in the form of a separate instrument. Such an arbitration agreement is equally binding on the parties as one embedded in the contract. In some national jurisdictions it might be asked whether the 'survivability' of arbitration provisions is the same under these two approaches. Generally speaking, the intended result is the same: the parties have committed to arbitration.

Agreements to arbitrate, whether embedded in an underlying contract or concluded separately, may commit the parties to arbitrate a defined category of future disputes—typically, all disputes that might arise under the contract in which they are embedded or to which they refer. Sometimes, parties instead conclude an agreement to arbitrate one specific dispute. This is typically done in the context of a pre-existing contractual relationship, possibly at the end of one. Yet nothing is to stop parties, when entering a contract to establish a new commercial relationship, from embedding an arbitration clause that addresses some particular pre-existing dispute between them.

To illustrate the difference between a general arbitration provision, covering a defined category of disputes, and an arbitration provision addressing a particular dispute that already has arisen, let us consider extracts from two model arbitration clauses published by the London Court of International Arbitration (LCIA). First, an arbitration provision covering a defined category of disputes:

> Any dispute arising out of or in connection with this contract, including any question regarding its existence, validity or termination, shall be referred to and finally resolved by arbitration under the LCIA Rules, which Rules are deemed to be incorporated by reference into this clause.

And here is the LCIA's proposed clause for use after a dispute has arisen:

> A dispute having arisen between the parties concerning [...], the parties hereby agree that the dispute shall be referred to and finally resolved by arbitration under the LCIA Rules.

The variety of clauses aiming for a similar effect is practically limitless. Under either of the clauses above, and a great many like them, the moment two parties adopt one, they have consented to arbitration on its terms.

The steps for establishing consent are often more complex in so-called 'mixed' arbitration—arbitration where one party is a private investor and the other is a state. It still is possible for the two parties to agree to arbitration, for instance in a concession contract between the state and the foreign investor. But the first step is more often the conclusion by two states of a BIT. Each state in the treaty offers—typically subject to further qualifications—to arbitrate disputes brought by investors from the other state who have invested in its territory. Consent is completed when an eligible investor, subject to whatever further qualifications the treaty stipulates, brings an arbitration against the state and invokes the treaty. Sometimes, instead, a state adopts a piece of legislation that offers all foreign investors, or at least those meeting certain requirements, the possibility of arbitration; the consent to arbitration is completed when an eligible investor institutes (i.e. starts) proceedings against the state.

Here is an example of an arbitration clause from a BIT (Colombia and the UK are the Contracting Parties in this treaty):

ARTICLE IX

Settlement of Disputes between one Contracting Party and an Investor of the other Contracting Party

[...]

(3) Disputes between an investor of one Contracting Party and the other Contracting Party which have not been settled [amicably or by local administrative remedies], shall, after a period of six (6) months from the Notification of Dispute, be submitted to the local courts or to international arbitration if the investor concerned so wishes.

As can be seen, this treaty is the first in a series of steps that might lead to arbitration by an investor against a government. A large variation of arbitration provisions is found in the many BITs in force between states; the precise steps that they require are not all the same. Where national law opens the door for investors to arbitrate against a government, the steps vary from one law to another as well. Here is an example of an arbitration provision in a national investment law (South Sudan's):

Article 39. Dispute Resolutions

[…]

(4) Any dispute between an investor and the Government in respect of an enterprise to which this Act applies but not amicably settled may be submitted at the option of the aggrieved party to arbitration as follows—

a. in accordance with the rules and procedures for arbitration by the International Centre for the Settlement of Investment Disputes […]

Whatever the steps parties take to consent to arbitration, by consenting to arbitration they bestow power (jurisdiction) upon an arbitrator or panel of arbitrators to impose a binding decision on them. However, this is a strictly circumscribed power. The terms of the parties' consent stipulate the limits. These may include time limits: start points or cut-offs before or after which events are not a matter for the arbitrators to address. They may, and indeed in arbitration clauses embedded in contracts almost always do, limit jurisdiction to questions arising in regard to a particular contract. They may include other more or less exacting definitions of the particular dispute (or disputes) that the parties have agreed arbitration shall resolve.

A key concept in arbitration is that arbitrators possess the power to interpret these limits of their powers: they have the competence to judge the limits of the competence that the parties have conferred, the limits of the parties' consent to jurisdiction. The French expression for this power, *compétence-compétence*, is in common usage in the arbitration community. Arbitrators, however, sometimes exceed the limits set out in the parties' consent. In a case of such *excess of powers*, an external check is available to the parties.

Instituting proceedings

Faced with a dispute that may be subject to arbitration, parties may wish to institute arbitral proceedings. With an arbitration agreement already in place that covers the dispute, it is not necessary for both parties to give a further consent for arbitral proceedings to start. All that is necessary is for one of them to invoke the arbitration agreement in conformity with whatever procedure that agreement indicates. The other party—often called the respondent—then is bound by law to participate in the proceedings and to respect the results.

Different arbitral procedures specify different ways to institute proceedings. Under some rules, notification is made directly to the other party. Under others, arbitral procedures are attached to a permanent institution, and that institution receives the request for arbitration. A prominent example of the latter is ICSID. Under the ICSID Convention, a party wishing to institute arbitration does so by writing to the secretary-general of ICSID and indicating the issues in dispute, who the parties are, and what the basis is for their consent to arbitrate. The secretary-general, under the rules of ICSID, has the power to throw out disputes that are 'manifestly outside' the jurisdiction of an ICSID tribunal. The secretary-general, however, exercises that power very infrequently. Many arbitral rules do not include such a threshold review power at all. We will return below to the role permanent institutions like ICSID play in the arbitration process.

Appointing arbitrators

An arbitration may be presided over by a sole arbitrator or by a panel of arbitrators. Arbitration panels (or 'tribunals') usually have three arbitrators, and in any case almost always an odd number.

Just as there are different procedures for instituting arbitration, there are different procedures for appointing arbitrators. The parties might agree for an arbitral institution to appoint a sole arbitrator. They might, instead, agree that they shall attempt to agree the sole arbitrator but specify an arbitral institution as a fallback appointing authority in the event that they fail to agree. In some arbitration provisions, the party that institutes proceedings is to appoint one arbitrator at the point in time when it communicates its request for arbitration; the respondent (the party being sued) is to appoint its arbitrator within some specified period of time thereafter (usually short, a month or less); and either the parties or the two arbitrators whom they have appointed are to agree to a chairperson or president. In any arrangement where the parties or their appointees are called upon to constitute an arbitral tribunal, the risk arises that one of them fails to appoint, or that agreement is not reached as to a chairperson or president. A well-conceived arbitral provision designates some procedure or authority to make appointments in case a party or the parties fail to. Commonly it is the arbitration institution administering the case which handles appointments in such situations.

Appointment provisions may be quite simple. For example, the American Arbitration Association proposes, among a number of alternatives, the following:

> Within 14 days after the commencement of arbitration, each party shall select one person to act as arbitrator and the two selected shall select a third arbitrator within 10 days of their appointment...If

the arbitrators selected by the parties are unable or fail to agree upon the third arbitrator, the third arbitrator shall be selected by the American Arbitration Association.

Some appointment provisions are more complex. The UNCLOS (see Chapter 1) provides for arbitration of certain disputes arising under the Convention. Its provision on appointments, which runs to eight paragraphs, provides for the constitution of an arbitral tribunal consisting of five members, one selected by each party and three by agreement; the parties are then to agree on the president of the tribunal from among those three. Fallback provisions for the case of the failure of a party to appoint, or failure to agree, refer the matter to the president of ITLOS, as the chief officer of a permanent court.

Some arbitral institutions maintain lists of individuals from which arbitrators may be chosen. A prominent example is the Permanent Court of Arbitration (PCA). Each country belonging to the PCA names to the PCA list a 'national group' consisting of four individuals. Parties who use PCA rules for an arbitration may then stipulate that their arbitrators are to be chosen from the PCA list. In keeping with the consent-based character of arbitration, however, they are also free to look elsewhere. An example of a more restrictive approach is found in the arbitration mechanism of FINRA (Financial Industry Regulatory Authority), a self-regulatory body concerned with the integrity of the American broker-dealer industry. Under FINRA's arbitration provision, parties are to choose from lists of ten potential arbitrators, the lists being drawn by computer algorithm from a larger roster maintained by FINRA. Once they have agreed to that provision, the parties choose arbitrators from the lists as prescribed.

Arbitral procedure

The variety of procedures that parties might choose for their arbitration is vast. To take just one of the many arbitral institutions, the American Arbitration Association has drafted specialized rules for different subject areas, such as construction, patent, and healthcare. The ICC has its Rules of Arbitration. A number of institutions have formulated procedures for expedited or 'fast-track' arbitration as an alternative when speed is of the essence. In principle, it is open to the parties to design a set of procedural rules from scratch. Parties seldom do so, however, precisely because well-tested procedures, such as those just mentioned, are available 'off-the-shelf'.

Typically at the first meeting following the appointment of the sole arbitrator or the constitution of the tribunal, the parties and the arbitrator(s) will address procedural issues specific to the case. Agreeing to the particulars of an arbitral procedure is usually one of the tasks at that meeting. Conferring with the arbitrator(s), the parties may adopt amendments or addendums to the standard, 'off-the-shelf' procedure. The parties have the opportunity in this way to refine pre-existing rules for the particular circumstances of their case.

Once the parties have given their consent to a particular procedure, that procedure applies equally between the parties. It further follows from the consent-based character of arbitration that, if the parties during the proceedings wish to amend the procedure, or if they wish to shape the manner in which the arbitrators conduct the proceedings under the agreed rules as those rules stand, it is open to them to do so. Many arbitrators boast that they are responsive to the needs of the parties. Management of the arbitral procedure is one of the main ways the arbitrators can be responsive. Naturally, changes made once an arbitration has begun must be with the consent of both parties.

The procedural rules applied by a tribunal suggest how the arbitration might unfold, at least in its general contours. As we are referring to ICSID later, we will use the Arbitration Rules of the ICSID Convention as an example.

The ICSID Rules begin by setting out in detail procedures for constituting the arbitral tribunal. The procedures include default mechanisms in the event of failures to appoint. They also address the possibility that a vacancy arises on the tribunal during the proceedings, and the situation where the parties have not agreed as to a method for constituting the tribunal. Under 'General Procedural Provisions', the Rules specify matters such as the making of procedural orders, preliminary consultations between the tribunal and the parties on procedure, the fixing of time limits for the various steps of the proceedings, and costs.

The ICSID Rules assume, subject to the parties agreeing otherwise, that the proceeding will have a written phase and an oral phase. The written phase consists of at least one exchange of written pleadings. Using the terminology of the standing international courts, including the ICJ, the ICSID Rules refer to the written submission of the moving party as a 'memorial'; of the responding party as a 'counter-memorial'. A second exchange takes place if the parties agree (a reply and a rejoinder).

Oral procedure under ICSID includes pleadings by legal counsel who represent the parties. It also may include testimony by parties, by witnesses, and by experts. The Rules provide for examination of witnesses, who appear under oath. As to documentary evidence, which can be submitted by the parties, the witnesses, and the experts, the Rules empower the tribunal to be the judge of its admissibility and its probative value.

In the proceedings, a number of ancillary procedures are available. A party may request provisional measures, whose purpose is to preserve its rights pending a final award. A party may also make preliminary objections, including objections that the dispute identified by the party instituting the arbitration does not fall within the arbitral jurisdiction to which the parties have consented. The Rules permit counter-claims, unless the parties agree not to allow them.

Where such ancillary procedures are started, the tribunal might organize the arbitral proceedings into separate phases to address matters such as preliminary objections before addressing the merits ('merits' meaning the substance of the dispute). Differences sometimes arise about important matters of procedure, including matters of evidence and whether to bifurcate proceedings between preliminary and merits phases. When such a difference arises, an arbitral tribunal might call on the parties to trade written arguments justifying their preferred solutions before it issues a short order resolving the difference.

Parties may choose an arbitral procedure that promises to be fast. They may choose an arbitral procedure that involves very little lawyering, even, in some examples, providing for the proceedings to go forward without legal counsel in the room. However, such streamlined procedures are practically never used in cases involving large sums of money. As the example of ICSID suggests, when a great deal is at stake in a case, the arbitral procedures that parties adopt are complex. The arbitral proceeding that ensues can take considerable time to complete.

In one crucial respect, arbitration, whatever the precise procedural rules, is very much like a well-functioning court: the arbitrators, like judges, are obliged to ensure fairness between the parties. Imbalanced treatment of party requests for evidence and witnesses, for example, are to be avoided. The parties are to be furnished equal time for argument. Any argument made, or evidence adduced, is to be open to rebuttal by the other side. So-called 'equality of arms' is a core principle in arbitration—though finding a mutually acceptable way to implement it can be challenging, especially where the parties come from different legal cultures. That said, the consent basis of arbitration assures, at least in theory, that the parties know what they are getting into.

The award

The arbitration panel, or the sole arbitrator, is required by the agreement of the parties to adopt an award that settles the legal questions presented by the dispute, to the extent that those questions fall within the jurisdiction that the parties have granted. The award is final and, in principle, without appeal. It is legally binding on the parties.

The section of an award that states the result in the case, including in particular the arbitrators' decision in regard to remedies (such as financial compensation), is referred to as the 'operative part'. This distinguishes it from sections of the award that recite procedural details or set out the arbitrators' reasoning. Here is an example, taken from a commercial arbitration, of the operative part of an award:

> For the reasons set out in detail above, the Tribunal makes the following Award:
>
> (1) Y shall forthwith pay to X the principal sum of US \$8,421,765.
>
> . . .
>
> (3) The ICC Court has fixed its administrative expenses and the fees of the members of the Tribunal as follows:
>
> Administrative expenses: US \$61,132
>
> Fee of the Chairman: US \$176,170
>
> Fees of the Co-arbitrators: (2 x US \$132,130) US \$264,260
>
> (4) The total expenses incurred by the Tribunal being US \$46,438, the total amount of the costs of the arbitration is US \$548,000.
>
> (5) The costs of the arbitration shall be borne by the parties equally . . .

Here is an example of the operative part of an award in an investment case, where, as it happened, the claimant, a rare earth minerals mining company, rather comprehensively lost against the government of Kenya:

> The Claimants' claims are dismissed with costs to the Respondent in the sum of US $3,226,529.21 plus US $322,561.14 in ICSID costs.

These examples by no means exhaust the possibilities of what an arbitral tribunal can order. Arbitrators might award specific performance, telling a party to do something, like release a consignment of raw materials that the other party paid for. They might award declaratory relief, declaring a legal finding, such as a finding that one party was in breach of patent rights held by the other party. In cases where financial compensation is ordered, the award often also orders interest. There is no general rule restricting what currency an award of financial compensation is expressed in, apart of course from the general rule that arbitrators shall defer to the parties' agreement.

Parties are free to agree about the overall form the arbitral award is to take. Especially in commercial settings, parties sometimes agree that the arbitrator or arbitrators need not set out legal reasoning: the decision is all they want. This streamlines the procedure and, probably, lowers costs, because an award without reasoning requires less time on the part of the arbitrators. It will not be acceptable to some parties, however, to have an award without an explanation. Therefore, in many arbitration agreements, and under some of the main arbitral institutions and the arbitration laws in many countries, arbitrators are required to include in the award the reasoning that led to their conclusions.

The reasoning set out in an award, in those arbitrations where reasoning is called for, addresses how the arbitrators decided the merits of the dispute. Among other matters that reasoning may address, one of the most important is the scope of arbitral jurisdiction. Even if the parties have not asked the arbitrators to express reasons, the arbitrators, in using their power to be the judge of the limits of their own competence, are still duty-bound to keep the award within the limits contained in the parties' consent.

A large body of reasoned arbitral awards has now emerged under particular rules systems. ICSID and UNCITRAL (the UN Commission on International Trade Law) are two prominent examples. It is not however completely agreed among scholars or practitioners to what degree past awards comprise something that approximates case law in a common law court. It is clear that past awards do not bind future tribunals. Yet arbitrators who are required to give reasons for their awards refer to past awards in their explanations. The basis of arbitration in the consent of particular parties suggests that past awards have only a limited role. However, the structure of legal reasoning in general and the desire to achieve predictable results lead arbitrators and legal counsel to pay considerable attention to the accumulated body of past awards.

Enforcing the award

Thanks to international treaties and conventions (especially the so-called New York Convention of 1958), arbitral awards are, generally speaking, easier to enforce abroad than court decisions. This is useful when the losing party holds far-flung assets and resists enforcement. The enforcement advantage is not uniform across all parts of the world. In particular, under the law of the European Union, the recognition and enforcement of court decisions is almost automatic between EU member states, and so there is perhaps less to be gained from rules requiring the enforcement of arbitral awards. Elsewhere, however, the enforcement advantage may be a key consideration favouring arbitration.

In an idealized picture of arbitration, the arbitrators adopt an award; and the parties obey. Enforcement of arbitral awards, however, is often a great deal less straightforward than that. We said above that arbitral awards, under most systems of arbitration, are not appealable. That does not mean that a final award is the end of legal proceedings.

Quality controls, challenges, annulments

A party in a national court proceeding in many cases has an opportunity to appeal the result. National law rules set down the procedures and substantive requirements for an appeal, and the court system is a permanent apparatus available to receive an appeal when a party properly lodges it. Arbitration, by contrast, prides itself in finality: the award, once rendered, is final and without appeal, except for very limited grounds of annulment (not appeal) relating to lack of power to decide the case and very serious procedural failures. Such challenges of an arbitral award are filed with the courts at the place of the arbitration, also called the 'seat' of the arbitral tribunal.

Arbitral tribunals come into existence to deal with just one specific case. At the moment an arbitral tribunal renders a final ruling in that case, like a bee that stings, it ceases to exist. Lawyers say that the arbitral tribunal that has delivered its final award is defunct—*functus officio*. Thus, not only are arbitral awards in principle not appealable; there is in practice (under most arbitration rules) nobody to appeal to. True, parties could give arbitrators an ongoing power of supervision of their affairs; but this is far from the normal practice. After the arbitrators have seen the case through, in the overwhelming majority of cases their power ceases.

The transitory character of arbitration tribunals has professional consequences for the people who serve on them. Courts, by contrast, are permanent institutions staffed by tenured judges—individuals appointed for a set period of time, for instance nine years in the case of the judges of the ICJ and for life in the case of the justices of the US Supreme Court. Judges such as these handle a great many disputes submitted to their court during their tenure. Arbitral tribunals are selected and appointed for just one dispute. Arbitrators who want to continue being arbitrators thus have to seek new appointments. Most are keen to get them, but there is no guarantee that they will. Not everyone agrees that this aspect of arbitration—private legal decision-makers for hire on a one-shot basis—is a good idea. They have an incentive to make decisions which please those who are most likely to appoint them again.

Some arbitration institutions contain permanent mechanisms for carrying out a limited review of awards. For example, the ICC has its International Court of Arbitration. As we noted earlier, this is not a court in the sense of a judicial body hearing and deciding cases. Instead, it is a standing body that performs a number of administrative and procedural tasks. Among its tasks is to monitor arbitral proceedings in order to assure that if the parties have chosen ICC Rules they are properly applied. The ICC Court also scrutinizes and approves final arbitral awards as a basic check on quality and to reduce the chances that a national court might decline to enforce. A more involved mechanism is the annulment procedure under the ICSID Convention, in which a party may apply for the full or partial annulment of an ICSID award by an ad hoc committee appointed by ICSID. There are only five grounds for annulment: improper constitution of the tribunal, manifest excess of power by the tribunal, corruption of an arbitrator, a serious departure from a fundamental rule of procedure, or failure to state reasons in the award. These grounds are all, broadly, oriented toward the process of arbitration. Annulment is not available for an error of fact or of law.

The New York Convention of 1958, an international treaty, provides a number of grounds on which a national court may deny recognition and enforcement of an award. A court may deny recognition and enforcement if the arbitration agreement was invalid or did not cover the dispute, the respondent was not properly notified of the proceedings, the arbitral tribunal was irregularly constituted, there was a serious procedural mishap, or the award had been annulled by the courts of the seat of the arbitration.

Thus, national courts, though they do not receive appeals from arbitration, nevertheless may be asked by a party to get involved. Most of the main commercial countries have adopted arbitration statutes that specify how and in what circumstances a national court can get involved. These statutes differ considerably among countries. The many countries that belong to the New York Convention are however under obligation to respect proper arbitral awards, subject to the possibilities the Convention sets out for a refusal.

The arbitration community keeps a watchful eye on how national courts treat arbitration awards. Any sign that the courts in a particular country are too ready to get in the way may scare off parties and counsel, who then will seat their arbitrations in other places, and thus shift the business there. Yet an approach by courts that is too lax might also be unattractive to parties: arbitration is a creation of party consent, but party consent, to be effective, needs a backstop in public law and public institutions. Not least of all, a safeguard must function to prevent overreach by the arbitrators, for the power of arbitrators to impose binding awards goes only as far as the parties' consent. Within the four corners of the arbitral process, the arbitrators possess *compétence-compétence*—the power under which arbitrators interpret the scope of jurisdiction—but an award that goes beyond the jurisdiction to which the parties objectively consented is and has to be susceptible to challenge.

Chapter 3 considers examples of how different types of parties use arbitration and concludes with an example of misuse of the kind that has provoked calls for more stringent external controls.

Chapter 3
The multiple lives of arbitration

Who submits disputes to arbitration today, and what are the disputes about? The diversity is great. It stretches from a consumer challenging an electricity bill from a utility company, to the utility company seeking compensation from a construction company for delays in completion of a nuclear power plant. From a manufacturer alleging that a competitor has breached its patent rights in a microchip, to a country alleging that its neighbour's armed forces have violated its maritime boundary. The claims parties make in arbitration also vary, from the mundane, such as that over an electricity bill, through to claims that are liable to provoke outcry—for example, a foreign investor demanding compensation from an underdeveloped country's government for financial losses arising from the COVID-19 emergency measures that that government imposed.

Even these examples cover only a sampling of the types of parties who have resorted to arbitration, and only a small slice of the variety of disputes that arbitrations have addressed. Given the many types of parties and diverse types of disputes involved, it comes as no surprise that, today, there is no one-size-fits-all model of arbitration.

Indeed many things vary across individual arbitrations, and there are as many ways to make sense of the overall phenomenon. The different boxes into which individual arbitrations can be placed could for instance bear the following labels: we could categorize them by the different permanent institutions that manage them; by the procedural rules that apply in the arbitration; by the substantive rules that apply; by the subject matter of the disputes that are arbitrated; by the opportunities for post-award review, and so on. In this book, we arrange them according to the types of *parties* that might submit disputes. It is a simple, intuitively understandable way to see the multiple lives of arbitration—and it is actually one of the main ways practitioners in the field sort themselves into sub-specialties as arbitrators and arbitration counsel.

First there are disputes, like the Alabama Claims, that pit two countries one against the other. We refer to these as 'interstate' or 'international' or sometimes 'intergovernmental' disputes. Then there are disputes between private parties: individuals in dispute with one another; individuals in dispute with companies; or companies in dispute with other companies. Legal scholars call these 'private' disputes. And, third, there are disputes between a private party, such as an individual or a company, and a government. In the field of dispute settlement, we know these types of disputes as 'mixed' disputes, because when such disputes are arbitrated the arbitrators decide a case that mixes parties of these two different kinds.

Interstate disputes are by definition international, even though some of the subject matters that states dispute over can also be the subject matter of disputes *within* a country, such as the location of a territorial boundary (see Box 1). Any dispute belonging to the second or third categories (private and mixed disputes) *could* be international. The individuals or companies in an arbitration of a private dispute might come from different countries; but you can also seek arbitration against a fellow citizen or a company from your own country: most private disputes take place within the borders of one country, and arbitration is employed to address a

Box 1 Intra-US interstate arbitrations

States of the US sometimes have agreed to arbitrate disputes between themselves. For example, the US states of Colorado and Kansas, under Article VIII of the Arkansas River Compact of 1949, agreed that certain disputes concerning their joint management of the river shall be submitted to arbitration. The century before, and on the other side of the country, Maryland and West Virginia arbitrated a dispute over the location of their boundary, which, it turned out in the arbitrators' award of January 1877, was on the southern shore of the Potomac river (see Figure 4). Interestingly, in arbitrations such as these, the states in dispute have sometimes applied substantive rules that resemble those used by countries when they adjudicate or arbitrate international boundary disputes. So these arbitrations are domestic, in the sense that the parties are from one country, but the rules applied to their disputes are, at least in part, informed by international law. In turn, countries arbitrating international boundary disputes have been known to look to cases from the US states for guidance.

4. The object of the 1877 arbitration: Harpers Ferry, West Virginia, as viewed looking south from the Maryland bank of the Potomac.

great number of such disputes. Arbitration between a private party and a government, likewise, might be international: the private party might be a citizen of Japan, and the government against which she is arbitrating might be that of Argentina. Although such *international* mixed arbitrations are those that the newspapers and scholars alike are most concerned with, mixed arbitration can be a strictly domestic affair: a government might agree to arbitrate certain issues arising between itself and one of its own citizens.

We are leaving to one side, for now, a proper discussion of the question of *applicable law*—that is to say, the question of what law the arbitrators are to apply when they arbitrate the dispute. In theory, the parties to an arbitration may stipulate any law they like. So two countries might agree to arbitrate between themselves and to apply the national law of one country. In theory. One seldom sees this in practice, however, because most interstate disputes involve issues of *international* law (think of Great Britain's obligation of neutrality in the Alabama Claims) and so, when arbitrating such a dispute, countries typically agree that it is international law that applies. Nevertheless, the choice of law is a matter that the parties to an arbitration control. Two countries in dispute with one another seldom choose a country's domestic law to govern their dispute. By contrast, two private parties often do, even when the two private parties are from different countries.

Before considering each of these three types of disputes more closely, we should clarify that any of these types of disputes might go to court, if the parties have not agreed to arbitration instead. Indeed, practically every dispute that might go to arbitration could go to court absent an agreement to arbitrate. The same does not hold the other way around however: not every dispute that might go to court might go to arbitration.

Arbitration of disputes between states

When countries have legal disputes with another, diplomacy is usually their first resort. This sets in motion negotiations at all government levels and typically is the best way to resolve interstate disputes, because it allows governments to maintain control over the outcome. But diplomacy does not always work. When diplomacy fails, governments sometimes submit their disputes to a third party for settlement.

After the Alabama Claims Arbitration, states began to encourage arbitration systematically. An early high point came in 1899, when the Hague Peace Conference, promoted by Russia's Tsar Nicholas II, produced the Hague Convention for the Pacific Settlement of Disputes. The Convention set up a new arbitral institution: the PCA (see Chapter 2). The PCA continues to this day—and in recent years has had a surge of activity.

So what exactly does the PCA do? The PCA is an organization that furnishes administrative services—a registry of sorts—for states, and sometimes other parties, that submit disputes to arbitration. The word 'court' in the PCA's title sometimes causes confusion, as does the fact that it shares a building with a real court: its secretariat and registry reside in the Peace Palace in The Hague, which is also the home of the ICJ (see Chapter 1), the principal judicial organ of the UN. The PCA, however, is not a UN organ, and it is not a court.

Parties to the PCA—119 of the states that belong to the UN are parties, as are Kosovo and Palestine—each appoint four eminent lawyers to be 'judges' of the PCA. These appointees are not employees of the PCA, and they do not act as 'judges' in the usual sense. Instead, they form a list from which parties to new cases are invited to appoint arbitrators. The parties are also free to appoint persons as arbitrators who are not on the list.

The PCA is the most active institution today for interstate arbitration. Some of its recent cases are described in Box 2. But it is not the only such institution. In the trade context, for instance, arbitrations take place between states to address alleged failures to respect international trade liberalization agreements. The WTO plays an important role in this area. But disputes under the WTO agreements are usually resolved through adjudication by specific WTO panels followed by an appeal to the WTO Appellate Body; not by arbitration. Then again, arbitration is possible there too: the WTO dispute resolution rules allow the parties to a dispute to resort to arbitration as an alternative to adjudication by panels and the Appellate Body. It is also possible to submit very specific sub-parts of a WTO dispute to arbitration, such as the question of what amounts to a reasonable time for implementing a WTO measure or authorizing suspension of concessions.

Box 2 The PCA in recent years

States in a number of disputes have agreed to use the PCA when they have arbitrated under Annex VII of the UNCLOS (see Chapter 1), the provision of that treaty providing for arbitration of certain maritime disputes. Examples include the *Mauritius* v. *United Kingdom* case concerning the waters around the Chagos Islands in 2015 and the *Philippines* v. *China* case concerning the South China Sea in 2016 (China, against the evidence, insisted that it had not really agreed to any such thing—and refused to appear in The Hague to argue its case). Outside the framework of multilateral treaties such as UNCLOS, states also have adopted freestanding agreements to arbitrate particular disputes and have chosen the PCA as registry. This is how Eritrea and Yemen agreed to arbitrate their dispute over the Red Sea islands in 1999. Croatia and Slovenia used the PCA in respect of a maritime delimitation dispute in 2017.

Trade-related disputes under other trade agreements have more commonly been submitted to arbitration. For example, under the North American Free Trade Agreement (NAFTA), Mexico instituted arbitration against the US in 1998 to challenge the legality of a US law that restricted Mexican trucking companies from operating in the US. The Secretariat constituted under NAFTA supplied management functions for the proceedings. Under the Softwood Lumber Agreement, the US instituted arbitration against Canada in 2007 in regard to certain aspects of a longstanding trade dispute over Canadian timber subsidies. The parties in that case used the LCIA (see Chapter 2). Like the PCA, the LCIA is not a court in the standard sense but, instead, an institution for hosting arbitrations when parties have agreed to use it.

Finally, states are free to agree to arbitrate without calling on the PCA or other similar institution to help manage the proceedings: they can opt for so-called ad hoc arbitration, an approach that does not involve any arbitration institution at all. However, more often than not, they do involve an institution. Arbitration institutions have a cadre of specialists, in the form of a permanent managerial staff, as well as physical premises suitable to hosting arbitral proceedings. The desire to avoid re-inventing the wheel is an incentive that leads states to use institutional arbitration.

Arbitration of disputes between companies or individuals

Private parties have resorted to arbitration with particular frequency when their disputes concern commercial matters. Sometimes they want to retain confidentiality and know that the courts cannot provide it, court proceedings generally being matters of public record. Sometimes they need technical experts to decide their case, not generalist judges. In some situations, one or both parties do not have confidence in the neutrality or even-handedness of the courts; one party is foreign or 'from out of town' and wishes to deny the other party a 'home court' advantage. There are any number of reasons why parties agree to keep their disputes away from the public court system.

Granted, the overall number of cases between companies or individuals resolved by arbitration is still only a fraction of the total; some estimates are that at least 300 times as many commercial disputes go to court as go to arbitration. Yet today there are roughly as many arbitrations filed each year with the ICC (see Chapter 1) as there were over a period of fifteen years during the last century, with a 50 per cent increase in the last ten years alone. And the ICC is only one of many arbitral institutions specializing in private commercial disputes. Others have experienced a similar boom. Arbitration of private disputes is a growth industry, both across international borders and within individual countries.

Such disputes encompass any of the usual business disagreements, such as late delivery of goods or services, late payment, delivery of faulty or damaged products, difference of interpretation of a contract, defects in the construction of a building or facility, violation of copyrights and trade secrets, insurance claims, disputes over employment contracts, disputes between publishers and authors over delays in writing books, and many more. Almost any commercial matter between companies or individuals can be resolved by arbitration.

Even consumer disputes (when a private person buys something for his or her private use from a professional trader) can in certain countries be decided by arbitration. Such consumer arbitration has provoked controversy, because some say it denies consumers a fair hearing in court. The controversy has risen to the front pages, the *New York Times*, for example, having published a series of scathing articles in 2015 about the supposed evils of consumer arbitration. (Employment arbitration got its share of blame too.) We will return later to some of the issues raised when large companies include arbitration clauses in the contracts that individual consumers routinely enter into—and seldom read.

A century ago, there were about a dozen institutions providing services in support of commercial arbitration. Today, there are too many to give a confident count: estimates vary between a few hundred and 1,000 commercial arbitration institutions in 2020. Commercial arbitration, however, is heavily concentrated in a small number of these. Around twenty-five institutions handle nearly all of the world's arbitration caseload.

The most prominent arbitration institutions are, in addition to the Court of International Arbitration of the ICC, the LCIA, the China International Economic and Trade Arbitration Commission (the world's largest by the number of disputes arbitrated, but most of them are quite small, domestic cases), the American Arbitration Association in New York, the Stockholm Chamber of Commerce, the Milan Chamber of Commerce, the Hong Kong International Arbitration Centre, and the Singapore International Arbitration Centre.

Arbitration is a global business. Many cities seek to attract arbitration, partly for the business value of arbitration in its own right, partly to foster a professional ecosystem congenial to overall economic development. But just as a relatively small number of institutions handle most of the world's commercial arbitration, this type of dispute settlement is heavily concentrated in a small number of places. London and Paris are the two most prominent places for commercial arbitration. Geneva is an important destination; Singapore has gained considerable ground in recent years. Various regional centres have appeared on the scene, with varying degrees of success.

Arbitration of disputes between a private party and a state

Investment arbitration has a geopolitical aspect: recall the crisis following the nationalization of the Anglo-Iranian Oil Company in Iran, and the World Bank's efforts in the aftermath to develop a dispute settlement mechanism that protects investors, while also respecting the sovereignty of developing and underdeveloped countries. So a few words are in order about *international* arbitrations between a private party and a state, before we turn to a rather curious case from France, in which a private investor was pitted against his own government—that is to say, a case of *domestic* mixed arbitration.

For a long time, if you had an investment overseas and you had a dispute concerning your investment with the local government, you had, in essence, two choices for pursuing a remedy, neither of them very desirable.

You could sue the local government in its own courts. This is not a promising course of action for an investor who has reason to believe that the local government already has the cards stacked against him.

The second option was to go to your own government and ask it to take diplomatic steps in order to obtain reparation from the alleged transgressor. This second option is known as 'diplomatic protection'. Diplomatic protection has a centuries-long heritage and is a practice by which one sovereign (originally, a prince or king) espouses a claim that one of its citizens has against another sovereign and, by making diplomatic representations to that other sovereign, seeks something to make good the injury that its citizen has sustained. Diplomatic protection is a less-than-perfect solution for a number of reasons.

For one, it is not easy convincing a government, even your own, to move the ship of state to serve your needs in an imbroglio with another country. A small company may well rise or fall on an investment it made abroad, yet the company's fate is a mere trifle in the government's hectic agenda. Faced with the choice between leaving you to your luck and upsetting its international relations with the foreign government, your government might well choose the former.

Even when you do convince your government to espouse your international claim, they are likely to bargain away a large part of it, for the same reason they might ignore you in the first place: governments have complex internal politics and wide-ranging responsibilities. A single citizen, even a large corporate citizen, cannot rely on the government to prioritize a diplomatic protection claim in face of the crosswinds that assault government decision-makers every day. Even when a government follows through to a settlement of some kind, the settlement is likely to be at a sharp discount against an amount that would actually repair the injury.

The French energy giant EDF experienced the limits of diplomatic protection, even though EDF is one of France's most influential companies. In 2009, EDF and its Italian peer ENEL had created a joint venture to conduct feasibility studies for the construction of at least four nuclear reactors. However, following a referendum in 2011, Italy backed out of new nuclear power projects. The EDF–ENEL reactor deal was called off. EDF, having already invested in the now-cancelled joint venture, called on the French government to demand reparation from Italy. EDF, though a private company, has the French government as its largest shareholder. Even so, the French government was reticent: there was too much else at stake between France and Italy for EDF's grievance to get in the way. (For example, France wanted Italy's help with illegal border-crossings after the Arab Spring led to an influx of refugees.)

Another problem with diplomatic protection is that your state, out of respect for the other state's sovereignty, is likely to refrain from exercising it until the other state's courts have had a chance to address your dispute. This leaves you with the original problem: the other state's courts. Indeed, if you dutifully turn to them, in order to show your own government that you tried, the local courts might deliberately delay. Thus, in turn, diplomatic protection by your own government could be delayed.

Enter international investment arbitration, which purports to avoid these problems. International investment arbitration, like the other forms of arbitration, comes in many shapes. In all its shapes, it is based upon consent. Among the ways that states might give consent to investors suing them in arbitration, the three we saw earlier account for practically all the cases: the investor and the government have a contract providing for arbitration; the investor's government has entered into a treaty, typically but not always bilateral, with the foreign government and that treaty provides for arbitration; or a country has enacted national legislation, often called an 'investment code', which gives foreign investors the right to sue the government in arbitration. In all three situations the right for the investor to initiate the arbitration may be subject to limitations expressed in the contract, treaty, or legislation. However, those limitations do *not* include a requirement that the investor consult with its own government. The right to arbitrate is held by the investor in that investor's own name. In this way, investment arbitration departs significantly from the old practice of diplomatic protection. It removes the investor's state from the process by giving the investor an independent right to arbitrate against the other state.

Whichever of the three ways is involved—contract, treaty, or national legislation—states consent to arbitration *before* disputes arise. And all three, in effect, put the investor on an equal legal footing with the foreign country against which the investor makes a claim. In theory, states could also consent to arbitration *after* a dispute has arisen, but in practice they virtually never do. The great majority (over 70 per cent) of the roughly 1,000 investment arbitration claims that have been filed in the last forty years were based on the consent states have given by signing BITs, most of the rest by entering into contracts with arbitration clauses or adopting national legislation that accepts investment claims.

Based on this short description, one might conclude that investment arbitration is a streamlined process. Compared to diplomatic claims, it is. Whether it is faster than court proceedings, however, depends on a variety of factors. Some investment arbitrations have dragged on for many years; others have concluded fairly quickly—within two or three years of the investor presenting its claims.

Investment arbitration is not necessarily cheap. International investment arbitration rules, for example those of ICSID, have procedures that are as complex as those found in court. Arbitration under such rules typically involves a great deal of lawyering—which means very large legal fees. It is one reason why international investment arbitration has become a coveted line of work for many of the largest law firms. It is also a reason for an investor not to form an expectation that an investment arbitration will be either very fast or very economical.

As mentioned earlier, mixed arbitration is not necessarily international. It can also take place in a domestic setting. It seldom does, but there was one mixed arbitration that gained notoriety in France and has influenced attitudes toward arbitration more widely. The case of Bernard Tapie provides an example of how a government might come to agree to arbitration in a dispute with one of its own citizens—and how a high-profile failure can generate public antipathy towards arbitration.

Bernard Tapie is a French citizen with a colourful career in business and politics. At a time when he was one of the twenty richest people in France and his business ventures were used as case studies in universities, Tapie bought Adidas, the sports equipment and apparel company. He sold his holdings in Adidas two years later, making an 80 million euro profit. However, he soon accused the state-owned bank Crédit Lyonnais, which had handled the sale of Tapie's holdings, of having defrauded him. According to Tapie, the bank had carried out a sale which was in fact larger by 390 million euro than Tapie was aware—and had cut him out of the profits. A legal battle erupted between Tapie and Crédit Lyonnais, which, because the bank was state-owned, for practical purposes involved Tapie in a contest against the French government. This started in 1995.

Twelve years later, in 2007, with the dispute still winding its way through the courts and with no end in sight, the French government agreed to Tapie's request to submit the Adidas problem to arbitration. Ostensibly, the idea was to bring the dispute to an end, which the courts had failed to do. But the circumstances in which the arbitration agreement was reached between Tapie and the government raised questions. To begin with, the newly elected President Nicolas Sarkozy had received financial backing from Tapie for his presidential campaign. Christine Lagarde, finance minister at the time, oversaw the conclusion of the arbitration agreement between Tapie and France, which included the approval of the selection of the three arbitrators who were to form the arbitral tribunal. It later emerged that the arbitrator who wrote most of the tribunal's award—a decision to order the French state to pay Tapie 400 million euro—had financial ties to Tapie and his lawyer. Yet Lagarde and her chief of staff, on behalf of the French state, were adamant that the government not initiate annulment proceedings against the award, against the opinion of their advisers that avenues for review should be explored. Lagarde later came under formal investigation by French authorities for her role in the Tapie matter, and her conduct was eventually found to have been negligent.

In 2015, with a new government in power, review of the award was at last sought. The Court of Appeal of Paris ruled on a motion for revision of the award (a special procedure, used because the French state had failed to initiate normal annulment proceedings within the time limit). The Court judged that the decision of the arbitral tribunal had been tainted by fraud; the award was retracted. This opened the way for the matter to be tried again in court. Tapie was soon ordered to pay back the 400 million euros he had received from the government under the arbitral award.

Critics of arbitration point to examples such as the Tapie affair to make a case that arbitration is a shady system that enables private parties and governments to breach the public trust. Champions of arbitration plead that one or two idiosyncratic cases, however deplorable the abuses they expose, do not represent the system. Yet arbitration, as a system, across all the different forms that arbitration takes, presents in one of its core features a risk of improper conduct. The independence of arbitration from the courts and from processes of appeal is a core feature of arbitration and one of its main supposed virtues. That very independence makes arbitration attractive to parties who do not wish too much light cast on their motives, methods, or goals. It also entails that even high-minded parties and conscientious arbitrators may not be in harmony with values and policies that society at large wishes to protect or promote, thus earning its occasional epithet of a 'justice bubble for the privileged'. A handful of small cases settled by arbitration would not matter; but arbitration handles an already significant and ever-growing numbers of cases, some of which, even taken individually, affect matters of great public concern.

We will look in Chapter 4 at how the law attempts to place checks on arbitration—and consider further why some critics say the law should do more.

Chapter 4
Arbitration and the law

Arbitration, as we have noted, is privatized justice. It is a consent-based mechanism for settling disputes without going to court, which is a public institution. Arbitration, however, does not exist in isolation from the law and the public institutions that apply and enforce the law.

An important consequence of the contact between arbitration and the law is that not all disputes are permitted to be arbitrated. The word lawyers use to describe disputes that the law permits parties to submit to arbitration is 'arbitrability'. Disputes that the law does not permit parties to submit to arbitration are said to be 'non-arbitrable'. The withholding by law of certain subject matters from arbitration reflects a widespread understanding that some decisions, for social or political reasons, should remain the province of government, that the resolution of certain disputes should not be 'privatized' by arbitration.

Parties who have agreed to arbitrate their dispute are affected by the law in other ways as well. For arbitration to function, the parties count on at least certain basic rules applying to their proceedings whether or not the parties have expressly chosen those rules. In this chapter, we consider how the parties to an arbitration count on the law and how they can choose the law that applies in their arbitration. Then we return to this question of

arbitrability, of which disputes the law will not allow to be
arbitrated.

Counting on the law: how legal rules support arbitration

What would happen if you had an arbitration agreement with a
customer, you sought to apply the agreement in order to pursue
the customer for unpaid invoices, but the customer refused to
appear at the proceedings? And what if the customer filed a
counter-claim against you (alleging, for instance, that the services
you provided were sub-standard)—and filed that counter-claim in
court rather than before the arbitrator whom you have appointed
in conformity with your agreement and whom your agreement
expressly empowers to deal with such a counter-claim? This is
the type of situation in which parties count on the law to support
arbitration.

There was a time when national law was, at best, ambivalent
toward arbitration. There were few countries with laws to enforce
arbitration agreements or to secure the abstention of courts from
hearing disputes submitted to arbitration. In some places, the
law was actively hostile to arbitration. The 20th century, however,
saw a pro-arbitration boom. Legislatures began adopting laws to
support arbitration. Two major examples of such laws are the
Federal Arbitration Act of 1925 in the US (still in force today, as
amended) and the Arbitration Act 1996 in the UK (which
re-stated and modified earlier UK arbitration laws). Today,
legislation, in almost all major commercial countries, empowers
and requires courts to support arbitration in various ways.

Three forms of support in particular merit consideration. First, if
a party fails to respect an arbitration agreement as in the situation
described above, a court may entertain a request to order the party
to arbitrate or to reject any suit that that party might have brought
to court in an attempt to bypass the arbitration agreement.

The court typically would command that both sides take their dispute to the arbitrator. In other words, the court would enforce an agreement to arbitrate. The legal system at large in this way supports arbitration. The legal system can be called upon to make sure that disputes that are subject to an agreement to arbitrate in fact go to arbitration; it keeps disputes that are subject to arbitration out of court.

Second, having compelled arbitration of a dispute and kept that dispute out of court, the law may allow parties to an arbitration to call upon the courts to lend assistance to the arbitral proceedings. During the course of arbitral proceedings a party may request courts and other public authorities to lend assistance in various ways. An example of assistance that a party might request is an order by a court to the other party to produce evidence relevant to the arbitration. Or perhaps the arbitrators have called on a person to attend the hearings in order to testify about things he witnessed. If the person ignores the arbitrators' summons, then they may ask a court to compel his compliance or to make a finding of contempt, much as the court would do if a witness neglected or refused a summons to appear in court. Arbitrators have no apparatus of their own to compel a party to do, or refrain from doing, any particular thing outside the arbitral proceedings. And, so, an order from a court can be a valuable aid to arbitration.

Third, once the proceedings have concluded, an award has been made, and the award has not been set aside during annulment proceedings in court, the legal system will assist a party in enforcing the award. Because the award is legally binding, a party whom the award addresses (e.g. to pay US $100,000 in money damages, to cease violating the other party's patents, to relinquish custody of a ship) should need no reminder that it is obliged to do what the award commands. However, in reality, losing parties do not always cooperate. And, as noted above, the arbitral tribunal has no apparatus to compel either party to do (or refrain from doing) any given thing. Another way in which the legal system at large supports arbitration is by lending its authority—and the public enforcement apparatus, such as bailiffs and the police—to compel a recalcitrant party to respect the arbitral award. Legal systems indeed largely equate arbitral awards to judgments of courts. In short, arbitrators exercise power by virtue of a private agreement, but parties can call upon public institutions through the courts to enforce their awards.

The availability of courts to enforce arbitral awards gives the winning party a powerful tool. To give an example of how that tool can be used, Charles Adams, an American-born arbitration lawyer practising out of Geneva, had argued and won a substantial award for a European client over the provision of high-speed rail technology to a consortium of Taiwanese companies. Courts in Taiwan failed to help when asked, mainly because Taiwan is not a party to the New York Convention of 1958. But Adams knew that in many other countries the authorities *would* help—and that one of the members of the Taiwanese consortium was a maritime transport company which owned and operated many ships. So Adams's next step: watch the Taiwanese company's ships until one of them pulls into the right port. Using publicly available intelligence on shipping traffic, Adams and his team watched. And soon enough the then-largest container ship in the world docked in Le Havre, France, loaded with valuable cargo of all kinds, including perishables. Within hours a taxi arrived in Le Havre, delivering a team of Adams's associates from the Paris office of his firm, with a certified copy of the award, the required stamp from a Paris court (called a stamp of exequatur), and an order of seizure of the ship. With little further ado, the port authorities arrested and impounded the vessel. With that asset now at stake, the Taiwanese consortium paid compensation to Adams's client as the award obliged.

Thus, a party may use the law, and the public institutions entrusted with enforcing the law, to enforce an agreement to arbitrate—all the way through to the enforcement of an award that arbitrators have adopted under the agreement.

However, not every agreement to arbitrate is supported by the law. For example, the Federal Arbitration Act in the US does not empower courts to stay litigation and compel arbitration in regard to certain contracts of employment. Thus, as the US Supreme Court said in 2019, a 'private agreement may be crystal clear and require arbitration of every question under the sun, but that does not necessarily mean the [Federal Arbitration] Act authorizes a court to stay litigation and send the parties to an arbitral forum.' So the public power is available to help with arbitration—but it is available on limited terms, terms dictated by the law.

So far, we have been considering how national law supports arbitration. There is no uniform international rule that tells countries in detail how they are to regulate arbitration. We have given examples to illustrate in broad brush how the law supports arbitration in the major commercial countries—but other countries may, and some do, take a very different approach, typically more restrictive in their support of arbitration. If these differences were left unchecked and went too far, they would jeopardize the core modern idea of arbitration as a global system of justice available for global transactions.

Arbitration has deep roots in international law and international relations. It accordingly comes as no surprise that countries, to address problems that differences between national approaches might cause, have adopted international solutions.

Some of the most important solutions are contained in the New York Convention of 1958. The New York Convention, the full title of which is 'Convention on the Recognition and Enforcement of Foreign Arbitral Awards', was concluded at a UN diplomatic conference, and today it applies to 163 countries and territories. It is one of the cornerstones of arbitration. The New York Convention requires national courts to support arbitration. First, under the Convention, when a court is presented with a case that the parties have validly agreed to arbitrate, the court must refer the case to arbitration. Second, it provides for the recognition and enforcement of arbitral awards that have been made in the territory of a state other than the state where the recognition and enforcement is sought. The Convention does not address how a given country deals with an award that results from an arbitration of a strictly domestic character within that country's jurisdiction. That is a matter for domestic law. It instead addresses, as its title suggests, *foreign* arbitral awards.

The Convention leaves it to domestic law and institutions to work out precisely how they will enforce agreements to arbitrate, including how they will assure that foreign arbitral awards are respected. It does not dictate specific national rules or procedures. It does, however, impose international obligations, binding on the countries that are parties to it. A country that is party to the Convention is not free to let its courts adjudicate disputes that have been properly submitted to arbitration, and as far as concerns arbitral awards made in other countries, that country is obliged to recognize and enforce them.

Choosing a law

Stopping court procedures that parties have opted out of by agreement, compelling arbitration that parties have opted into, lending assistance in the conduct of arbitral proceedings, and enforcing arbitral awards are all ways that the law supports arbitration. But what about the rules to be applied to the substance of the parties' dispute? Who supplies the rules under which the arbitrators determine the outcome of the case?

Recalling that arbitration is a process of private dispute settlement, one might surmise that parties who have agreed to arbitrate a dispute have to make up their own law. Parties are indeed free to invent any legal rules they wish, within limits that we will touch on. However, in the overwhelming majority of arbitration agreements, parties designate a particular existing set of rules and stipulate that these are the rules that will apply to the substance of their dispute. They will for example choose English law, or Danish law, or Australian law as the law that the arbitrators shall apply to the merits of the case before them (i.e. to the substance of the parties' dispute). When the parties have chosen well, the law that they have chosen addresses the substance of their dispute in sufficient detail and with sufficient clarity to give an answer to any merits question that might arise in the case. Most likely, the parties will do some bargaining about choice of law, and that is part of the attraction of arbitration: it entrusts this choice, as well as so much else, to the agreement of the parties.

The law applicable to the merits of the case does not have to be the same as the law applicable to the *procedure*. For example, the parties might choose the law of Sweden to govern their commercial contract and the substantive decision to be reached under an arbitration arising under that contract, but they might choose the law of Singapore to govern arbitral procedure. This choice of law would mean that a substantive question in a dispute—such as what quality standard the provider of a consignment of machine tools is obliged to meet—will be settled under the law of the underlying contract (Swedish law in this example); procedural questions—such as what interim measures of protection, if any, are available from the tribunal prior to a final award—will be settled under the law governing the procedure (Singaporean law in this example). The parties very well might choose the *same* law for the merits and for procedure; but there is no general rule requiring that they do. Often different laws are chosen.

Parties in fact seldom expressly name which country's law applies to the procedure of their arbitration. Typically what they name is a 'seat' of arbitration. The arbitral seat is a given place, and by virtue of having been named the seat, the law of that place applies to the procedure of the arbitration. Naming the seat also triggers the jurisdiction of the courts at the seat, so that it is to those courts that a party turns if wishing to challenge the award in annulment proceedings. So, for instance, when the parties choose Geneva as the seat, this means that Swiss arbitration law will govern the procedure of their arbitration, and that the Swiss Federal Tribunal will verify that this law has been properly followed if one of the parties argues that it has not.

The seat of an arbitration is usually the physical location where the arbitral proceedings take place. However, the proceedings may take place somewhere other than the seat. The seat of arbitration is a legal anchor, analogous in some ways to a place of incorporation of a company that may, or may not, host the physical assets or activities of the company. An arbitration with its seat in Geneva legally takes place in Geneva, but where it physically takes place—where the lawyers meet, where the hearings happen—can be anywhere the parties choose, even in 'cyberspace' when the hearings are conducted by videoconference.

The arbitration law of the seat of the arbitration often is not very detailed. It therefore might need to be complemented and specified. The typical way that this is done is with the rules of the arbitration institution that administers the arbitration. For instance, an ICC arbitration (i.e. an arbitration administered by the ICC) is conducted under the arbitration rules of the ICC, to the extent that those rules complement or specify the rules of procedure provided by the arbitration law of the seat. If the parties do not want to involve an arbitration institution, then they might use template procedural rules. To give one of the main examples, UNCITRAL adopted Arbitration Rules in 1976, which have been revised several times over the years. In their latest form, the UNCITRAL Arbitration Rules, in forty-three articles, set out rules of procedure that parties may elect to govern the conduct of an arbitral proceeding.

Though many options exist for the parties regarding choice of law, in practice the typical arrangement is that the seat of arbitration is also the physical location where the proceedings take place—meaning that the law of the physical location is the procedural law of the arbitration. Also, though the parties may choose any substantive law that they wish for the arbitrators to apply to the merits of their dispute, it is typically the substantive law of their underlying contract that applies—meaning that the law that governs the substance of the parties' business or other relationship is the law that the arbitrators apply in order to decide the dispute.

Must parties choose a national legal system to govern their arbitration? Commercial parties normally will do so, but they are not obliged to. When it comes to interstate arbitrations, as we have seen, the parties, which are both countries, are likewise free to choose the law they wish, but they choose international law in the vast majority of cases, and perhaps a particular treaty or treaties, as the substantive law for their arbitration.

Notwithstanding the prevalence of these approaches that we have just described, parties to an arbitration agreement might opt out of legal rules altogether. Parties may, if they agree, settle a legal dispute by applying a decision-making rule that is not a legal rule at all. For example, parties could agree that the dispute will be settled by a throw of two dice or by a pronouncement of an artificial intelligence. It is hard to imagine a present-day commercial party accepting decision-making rules such as those. However, it is not unheard of for parties to agree to an equitable approach. That is to say, instead of applying substantive legal rules to the substance of their dispute, they empower the arbitrators to reach a decision on the basis of equity. Parties thus call for settlement of their dispute *ex aequo et bono*—'according to the right and good'—instead of according to any particular substantive law source. Such an approach, which calls on the arbitrators to consider overall fairness rather than to apply specific rules of decision, is recognized by national legal systems and in international law, including in the Statute of the ICJ.

There are also various other systems that contain substantive rules and that are more or less law but are neither national nor interstate. In particular, numerous ecclesiastical or religious systems provide rules to govern certain transactions and human relations (see Box 3). Parties to an arbitration agreement—subject to legal rules meant to protect the public interest, which in many countries limit such choices—may choose systems like those to govern their disputes.

What disputes cannot go to arbitration?

Not all differences can be expressed as legal questions. It is also the case that not all legal questions can be solved by arbitration. Practically every country has laws that require its courts to address certain disputes that are brought to them, and, accordingly, the law forbids parties from opting out of court to settle those disputes by arbitration.

What types of disputes does the law withhold from arbitrators? National law plays a role here, and national law differs from country to country. It is impossible to supply a precise single list of disputes that is neither overinclusive nor underinclusive for some countries. Speaking in generalities, one can say that criminal matters are excluded from arbitration. Few if any states will allow private decision-makers to adjudicate questions of criminal law. Thus, if somebody stands accused of murder or manslaughter, robbery or embezzlement—any charge that gives rise to criminal jeopardy—the law does not let the prosecutor and the accused hand the case over to an arbitral tribunal. The exclusion of criminal matters from arbitration accords with the character of arbitration as a tool for regulating *private* disputes and with the

Box 3 Arbitration and the Sharia law debate

In the UK, among other countries, politicians, lawyers, and social commentators have debated in recent years how religious law might apply within a plural society. Sharia law institutions have attracted the most attention, but the question applies to dispute settlement under the laws of other religions as well. Arbitration figures centrally in the question: what disputes is a society willing to allow its members to submit to arbitration under religious law, and what safeguards in the form of public oversight should the public law provide?

When it comes to their ordinary commercial disputes, there is little controversy that parties should be free between themselves to consent to arbitration under religious law. The controversy arises when religious-based arbitration starts to affect core public values, like legal equality between the genders. Baroness Cox, in the UK House of Lords, referring to Sharia as well as to religious tribunals generally, advised not to foster 'the development of a parallel quasi-legal system based on inherently discriminatory principles', the concern being in particular that 'many women suffer from gender discrimination in these contexts'. And yet it was also important to have an arbitration policy that 'does not interfere in the internal theological affairs of religious people. If people wish to submit voluntarily to the rulings of any body, religious or otherwise, even if that means surrendering their rights under English law, they are free to do so' (House of Lords, 19 October 2012, col. 1684).

A Muslim arbitration tribunal in the UK offers its services, *inter alia*, in Islamic divorce, inheritance law, and Islamic wills. The United Synagogue in London hosts a beth din—rabbinical court—which, among other matters, deals with divorce under Jewish law. The extent to which national law respects religious arbitration differs from country to country. And, of course, there are countries where the religious law *is* the public law, but that is another matter.

character of criminal law as a tool for regulating relations in society at large.

States traditionally have also been cautious about letting arbitrators decide matters of family law. Divorce proceedings and proceedings to determine paternity thus have often been excluded from arbitration. In the event a marriage breaks up, the parties might prefer to have their own chosen decision-maker decide who obtains custody of the children, but this is a type of legal question that most legal systems, until recently, have not been comfortable allowing parties to entrust to private judges. The precise extent of the limits on arbitration in this regard varies from one country to another: France, Germany, and Quebec, for instance, still impose wide prohibitions over the arbitration of divorce matters, whereas the English courts have become much more liberal over the last decade in allowing family matters to go to arbitration, now excluding only matters such as the international relocation of children and child protection proceedings. In California, which is probably closer to the international average, questions of property division and spousal support can be decided in arbitration, but child custody arrangements cannot.

Arbitrability and non-arbitrability correlate with the commercial or non-commercial character of the dispute: commercial disputes are generally arbitrable; non-commercial disputes are generally not. This is only a rough proxy however for the careful analysis needed when arbitrability is in doubt. In particular, one needs to look closely at national law and judicial practice, because one country's idea of a run-of-the-mill commercial case well might be another country's idea of a matter of high public interest that no private arbitrator should ever touch. Most legal systems define 'commercial' broadly enough to respect a wide range of private agreements to arbitrate.

Also suggesting the limits of a simplified taxonomy, in some countries, competition or anti-trust issues, though clearly involving commercial affairs, are deemed too important for society to allow arbitrators to address. Determining the validity of a patent (as distinct from determining rights under patents that are established as valid) is a public function, and major jurisdictions, including the Netherlands, Germany, France, and China, do not let arbitrators decide patent validity claims. The US allows a limited exception: arbitrators may determine patent validity *as between parties in the arbitration*; other parties (i.e. the public at large) are not bound by the arbitrators' determination. This approach to patent arbitration reflects the general proposition: to the extent that a matter is just between private parties, it can be arbitrated; but to the extent that the legal questions have an impact on others, on 'the public', the law may insist the case go to court. The differences among countries also illustrate why generalizations as to arbitrability must be approached with caution.

It is not the purpose of arbitration to settle every possible dispute that might arise concerning every possible enterprise. In particular, though a parallel system of justice, arbitration is not meant to promote parallel markets that evade public law or values. (See also Box 4.) An attempt at such evasion gave rise to a landmark case in the 1950s. An Argentine businessman and a French company had arranged that one was to pay the other a commission (tens of millions of dollars in present-day terms) in exchange for a major public contract awarded by Argentina's government. The Argentine businessman was to see to it that the public contract would go to the French company. At some stage the businessman became ill and left the country. In his absence, the public contracts did not fully materialize, and so the French company refused to pay. The parties presented the matter as an ordinary commercial dispute and sought to resolve it through arbitration. The arbitrator discerned that the arrangement was, in truth, a scheme of bribery, not a valid commercial transaction. The case was declared non-arbitrable. According to the award, 'there exists a general principle of law ... that contracts which

Box 4 Arbitration and money laundering

For some twenty years, the arbitration industry has been aware that malign actors might exploit private dispute settlement to conceal illicit financial sources. For example, a drug smuggler generates millions in cash from his criminal activity. The smuggler is at risk when he attempts to spend or to invest those gains if he cannot give the appearance that they came from a lawful source. The smuggler thus seeks to 'launder' the money, a process by which it is passed through one or more institutions in order to obscure its source or, better yet for the criminal, to create a record seeming to show that the money came from a lawful source. The money laundering process involves any number of legitimate institutions such as banks and retail businesses. Imaginative criminal organizations figured out that arbitration is another legitimate institution that they might exploit for money laundering. The mechanism functions something like this: criminals set up two bogus companies; one initiates an arbitration against the other over a fake dispute worth the amount in need of laundering; the arbitral tribunal, wittingly or not, finds the claim has merit and awards the claimant the full sum. The losing party promptly delivers the money to the other's bank, arbitral award in hand to justify the funds transfer. The winning party declares the money to the authorities, explaining that it is the sum received as compensation through a successful claim in arbitration. The aim of money laundering thus would be achieved: creating the appearance that a lawful source exists to explain an illegal financial gain.

Improved banking regulations, the growing awareness of tax authorities, and guidelines for arbitrators have made such practices more difficult. The arbitration community, conscious of professional and civic responsibility, as well as of reputational

> risk, continues to be alert to the danger posed by the criminal
> misuse of arbitral proceedings. And the legal system, of course,
> does not allow arbitration for money laundering.

seriously violate *bonos mores* or international public policy are
invalid or at least unenforceable and that they cannot be
sanctioned by courts or arbitrators'. Though a system of privatized
justice, arbitration does not function in isolation of public
standards.

What if a dispute should not have gone to arbitration but did?
Arbitrators have the power to judge the limits of the parties'
consent to arbitration (*compétence-compétence*) but they do not
have the power to ignore those limits. If a party believes that an
arbitrator in handing down an award has exceeded her
competence, then the party might use the New York Convention
of 1958 to prevent the recognition and enforcement of the award.
In that case, the party would invoke Article V, paragraph 1(c), of
the Convention, which allows a court to deny recognition to an
award that deals with a matter 'not contemplated by or not falling
within the terms of the submission to arbitration' or a matter not
actually raised in the proceedings.

The New York Convention also recognizes challenges against
arbitral awards that deal with subject matter that the law does not
allow to be arbitrated. The relevant rule is found in Article V,
paragraph 2, of the Convention, which merits quoting in full:

> 2. Recognition and enforcement of an arbitral award may also be
> refused if the competent authority in the country where recognition
> and enforcement is sought finds that:
>
> (a) The subject matter of the difference is not capable of settlement
> by arbitration under the law of that country; or

(b) The recognition or enforcement of the award would be contrary
to the public policy of that country.

Sub-paragraph (a) reflects the idea that the law in practically
every country indicates some or another subject matter that
is simply not possible to settle by arbitration. Blanket exclusions
from arbitration—for example of criminal matters, exclusions
which as we noted are almost universal—thus are respected under
the New York Convention. So are exclusions from arbitrating
certain more specific subject areas. For example, Italy's Corte di
Cassazione (Supreme Court) in 2015 held that a contract between
Iraq and an armaments company for sale of military helicopters
was barred under the UN arms embargo (even though the
embargo was subsequently lifted), and, therefore, disputes over
that contract could not be resolved by arbitration.

Sub-paragraph (b) deals with the so-called 'public policy'
exception. Under the public policy exception, a court in a country
may refuse recognition and enforcement of an arbitral award if it
finds that to recognize or enforce would violate 'the public policy
of that country'. The concept of public policy is potentially
extremely wide. It exists however within limits defined by national
law. At the same time, because national law defines the limits,
they differ from country to country. A lawyer advising a client
whether a given arbitral award is likely to be recognized and
enforced therefore may need to consider how the law defines, and
how the courts interpret, the public policy exception in the
country (or countries) where the client might seek recognition and
enforcement.

A recent example of a court denying enforcement of an award on
public policy grounds involved a hydrocarbon company that had
prevailed in an arbitration against India. The company asked a US
court to order India, in accordance with the arbitral award, to
allow the company back into India's maritime area to carry out
natural gas exploration. The US court said that it would be

contrary to US public policy for a US court to order a foreign country to provide such a remedy, because to do so would in effect result in the US court 'exercising dominion over' that country. Courts around the world generally take a similar approach. Respect for the sovereignty of other states is part of general international law, and the principle of comity of nations also leads courts to take care before involving themselves in other countries' domestic jurisdiction. Caution in such matters, however, does not equate to complete abstention. Thus, a court in the US judged that American public policy supplied no reason not to order Russia to return certain texts and artefacts held in Russia that an arbitration tribunal in the USSR years before had awarded to a religious organization, now based in the US. In another case, a US court ordered Venezuela to respect an arbitral award indicating specific performance of a management agreement for a hotel in Venezuela. So even within one country the public policy exception is to be understood by referring to the specifics of the case at hand.

Courts in most countries are careful not to apply the public policy exception to excess. As we have noted, countries (and even cities) compete with one another for arbitration business, both because professional communities want that business and because being 'arbitration friendly' is said to foster a good economic climate overall. It is sometimes said that the risk that arbitration business will leave the locality is an unspoken consideration that stays the hand of judges who might otherwise be readier to interfere with an arbitration.

What about arbitration between states, as distinct from arbitration where private actors are party? Is there a requirement of arbitrability when it comes to interstate arbitration? Are there laws that apply to states when they have agreed to arbitrate a dispute, even when they have not expressly invoked those laws? Unlike private parties in one country, states on the international stage are not subject to a fully developed public law with an enforcement apparatus. Consent is the main limitation on whether states arbitrate against one another. Nevertheless, under international law certain rules, or at least certain principles, apply generally to all states, including when they arbitrate. There have for instance been hints that certain UN sanctions articulate non-derogable rules—and thus that a mixed private–state contract that ignores one of those rules would itself be void. We saw an example in the Italian Supreme Court case just noted concerning the Iraq helicopter contract and the UN arms embargo. Other examples might follow. The point remains that the arbitration agreement is of key importance, but it is affected in various ways by the surrounding law. This is so under national law and international law as well.

Chapter 5
The politics of arbitration against governments

'Justice should not only be done, but should manifestly and undoubtedly be seen to be done.' A British law lord penned this famous aphorism in the 1920s. Few are watching when arbitration involves private parties wrangling over fine points in a commercial contract. But when the claimant is a foreign company, often a large foreign company, and the respondent is a government, often the government of a developing or underdeveloped country, and when the claims are for billions, and the economy and the sovereignty of a country are said to be at stake, arbitration becomes front page news. Investment arbitration attracts far more attention than other types of dispute settlement. Accordingly, it is not necessarily enough that an investment award be a paragon of legal excellence. The award, and the whole institution surrounding it, must convince presidents, parliaments, and publics that justice indeed has been done.

Investment arbitration is not just a branch of legal practice in which a lawyer's technical sense of rule-based justice must be achieved. It is also an institution that has particular social and political effects. Accordingly, its wider justice implications on society and politics are starting to be studied with increasing attention in recent years. The results of these studies have in turn fortified public discussions around a 'crisis' of arbitration and a 'backlash' against its practice.

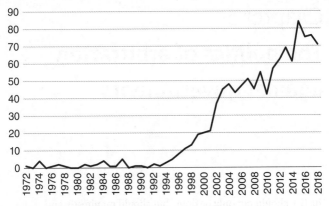

5. **Number of investment arbitration claims filed per year.**

Before we turn to the emerging critique of investment arbitration—and the backlash—let us remind ourselves of the reasons that investment arbitration has increased in frequency and continues to inspire admiration and support in many quarters.

Investment arbitration allows a private investor to sue a foreign government. Forty years ago, suits of that kind were practically unheard of (see Figure 5); their routinization was unthinkable. On average recently, by contrast, two new investment claims were being filed against a government each week. Diplomatic protection (the best an investor could hope for before investment arbitration came on the scene) was for most claimants a dismal consolation; governments usually have their own, and more important, matters to attend to. With investment arbitration, however, cautious diplomats and the remote calculus of statecraft no longer devalue the investor's claim. Investors now bring claims on their own, backed by platoons of corporate lawyers going in for the biggest feasible win. Governments that at one time could get away with uncompensated expropriations of foreign companies and rigged court proceedings have found themselves answerable under international law, thanks to investment arbitration. This was a rude and much-deserved awakening for countries accustomed to treating legal commitments as mere scraps of paper. If states hosting investments are unable or unwilling to provide the security of the rule of law, then investment arbitration fills the void. The international bar (the lawyers and law firms who built the system and run it) have thereby put legal chains on political power in situations that, only a generation ago, would have looked hopeless for investors. They have given investors unprecedented legal protection when they go abroad.

International legal standards have advanced hand in hand with investment arbitration. A government does not escape responsibility by saying that its own law or its own courts have declared a given abuse against an investor to be lawful. Investment treaties set out substantive protections, such as fair and equitable treatment, full protection and security, and a guarantee against discriminatory expropriation. There is a great deal of nuance, and controversy, as to what precisely the treaty protections mean, but what is clear is that they give investors legal rights independent of domestic rules that an unfriendly government might have manipulated at the investor's cost.

This is the story that investment arbitrators and the lawyers who practice before them like to tell. It is an impressive story, and it is no mere professional propaganda. Investment arbitration marks a great step forward for rule of law in international affairs. Investment arbitration's denizens rightly celebrate the achievement. And for a long time the world largely joined in the celebration.

Discontent, rising

Initially the discontent with investment arbitration was mostly limited to less developed countries. People in countries such as

Ecuador complained that the institution had eroded their sovereignty for the benefit of wealthy foreigners. Politicians in the most developed countries, however, have begun questioning investment arbitration as well.

In the US presidential election of 2016, neither candidate had warm words for investment arbitration. And indeed, the US-Mexico-Canada-Agreement (USMCA), concluded by the Trump administration to replace NAFTA, ended investment arbitration between US investors and Canada and between Canadian investors and the US. It also substantially reduced US–Mexico investment arbitration.

The discontent is not just American. Both the German and French governments said that they would scuttle the Transatlantic Trade and Investment Partnership (TTIP) if it contained investor–state arbitration (see Figure 6). The EU's trade commissioner in 2015, talking about TTIP on a visit to the US, declared ISDS (investor–state dispute settlement) 'the most toxic acronym in Europe'.

Nor is this shift towards a more critical view of investment arbitration limited to political circles. Such organs as *The Economist* and *Financial Times*, addressing financiers, professionals, and businesspeople, have raised questions about investment arbitration. The Cato Institute, an American think tank dedicated to limited government and free markets and a vocal defender of consumer arbitration contracts under the banner of freedom of contract, invokes national sovereignty in questioning the benefits of investment arbitration. Whereas opposition to arbitration is often associated with the political left, in the case of investor–state arbitration the opposition echoes across the political spectrum.

Why such a turn against investment arbitration? Is there something fundamentally wrong with it? Or is the problem one of

INVESTORS RIGHTS IN TTIP

MASSIVELY EXPANDING
THE REACH OF THE CURRENT ISDS SYSTEM

WITH TTIP   TODAY

28 EU countries could be sued, directly, compared to only **9** today

100% of US investment in the EU covered, compared to only **1%** today

51,495 companies could sue directly, compared to **4,500** today

6. Continuing resistance to the TTIP is fuelled, among other things, by an understanding that increased ISDS (another name for investment arbitration) will expand investor rights.

perception more than substance, nothing a better public relations plan would not fix?

For one thing, developed countries have been the target of investment claims considerably more in recent years than earlier had been the case. Figure 7 shows how prevalent investment arbitration against governments of developed states has become. Opinion-shapers and the general public have been surprised to learn of investment treaties that empower panels of arbitrators, who are unknown to the public and answer to no national

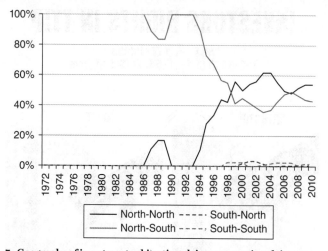

7. Geography of investment arbitration claims, comparing claims over time by region of claimant / region of respondent. Investment arbitration is increasingly used to target developed states, referred to here as the 'North'. About 130 of the world's nearly 200 countries have meanwhile been sued in investment arbitrations.

parliament, to adopt awards that seem to call into question the freedom of the state to manage its own affairs.

To take perhaps the most striking example so far, in 2011 Philip Morris launched an arbitration against Australia in which the company attacked health legislation that Australia had recently adopted to require anti-smoking labels on cigarettes. The company alleged (correctly, it would seem as far as it went) that the labelling law would depress the sale of cigarettes. It took the arbitral tribunal until the end of 2015 to decide that it could not deal with the issue because of a legal technicality. (The technicality related to Philip Morris having changed its corporate nationality in an attempt to find a treaty that would let it sue Australia.) Meanwhile, however, legislators in a number of other countries had become chary, postponing for years the implementation of similar anti-smoking measures, even though the World Health

Organization declared smoking 'one of the biggest public health threats the world has ever faced' and as of 2015 only 18 per cent of the world's population was protected by national smoke-free laws.

Arbitration had never before had such a political and social impact as it did in connection with countries' efforts to curb smoking. It was not designed to. And, yet, speculation already is rife, in mid-2020, that emergency health measures adopted in response to the COVID-19 pandemic are destined to come under attack by investors invoking the arbitration clauses of BITs. The visionaries who pushed for the development of arbitration to pacify the world and accelerate economic growth certainly never imagined that arbitration might be bad for public health.

Concern in the developed world also arises from the substantive trade agreements that often contain arbitration clauses. These agreements opened the developed countries' markets to goods from less developed countries, where labour, tax, and environmental rules are often less stringent, enticing companies to move their operations there. Communities in the developed countries suffered job losses at the time when manufacturing was moving abroad. Ohio, the British Midlands, and the Ruhr did not become 'rust belts' because of investment arbitration—but investment arbitration is provided for in the trade agreements that correlated to the challenges that those regions have faced. Unsurprisingly then, ISDS fell into the cross-hairs of trade unions and political leaders across the old industrial heartlands.

As for the less developed countries, investment arbitration came to look like it singled them out as the target of investors' suits. True, investment claims are not a one-way street; many developed countries have been sued under investment arbitration agreements. However, so many claims have resulted in major awards against less developed countries that the perception of discrimination took hold. An echo here is heard from very different areas of international law—not least, international criminal law—where the least developed regions have come in for the toughest scrutiny. The International Criminal Court (known by its abbreviation 'ICC', but not to be confused with the International Chamber of Commerce which arbitration lawyers refer to by this same abbreviation) has heard the preponderance of its cases against defendants from Africa, a disparity that African countries have protested. Criminal law and international investment law are different fields, but both have fomented discontent about their seemingly disparate impact on different parts of the world.

Trade-offs, good and bad

Arbitration, whatever its form, requires the consent of the parties. An arbitral tribunal will exercise jurisdiction over a country only if the country has consented for it to do so, which it can do through contract, treaty, and national legislation. States have, or at one time had, two main incentives to consent to investment arbitration.

First, in the days when powerful states were more ready to use coercive measures against weaker states, arbitration promised to be the antidote to problems that might otherwise provoke or become pretexts for intervention. Recall the crisis in Iran in the early 1950s, discussed in Chapter 1. The UK and the US might have refrained from orchestrating the coup d'état against Mossadegh if an effective legal remedy had existed to make the Anglo-Iranian Oil Company whole after Iran's expropriations. Investment arbitration is civilized justice, and civilized justice promotes peace. This is the theory of arbitration that was near and dear to the founders of the ICC in 1919.

But consenting to investment arbitration is a high price to pay for an unenforceable promise to refrain from an intervention that would be illegal anyway. Is it acceptable to concede the power that one's own courts heretofore have exercised to arbitrators, who belong to an elite of foreign legal experts—and all as a pay-off to a country that you probably view as an imperialist aggressor in the hopes it will not invade you? Even sixty or seventy years ago, such a calculus was dubious. Today, it hardly holds water at all. The most powerful countries hesitate to carry out interventions, armed or covert, except in carefully limited cases. Would one seriously believe that those countries refrain from interventions because arbitration clauses are in force? A study by Srividya Jandhyala of ESSEC Business School in Singapore, Geoffrey Gertz of the Brookings Institution in Washington, DC, and Lauge Poulsen of University College London confirmed the common-sense intuition: 'While the US government made extensive use of threats of military action, sanctions and aid withdrawals to compel host states to settle investment disputes in the 19th and 20th centuries, there is little evidence of such coercive diplomacy during the contemporary period.' And the evidence suggests that the availability of investment arbitration has nothing to do with the decline in coercion: 'Whether or not an investor has access to treaty-based investment arbitration appears to make little difference to how strongly the US government applies diplomatic pressure to resolve the dispute.' Maybe consenting to investment arbitration was once a type of self-defence for weaker states. There is no evidence that it serves any defensive purpose today.

Suitably, advocates of investment arbitration seldom describe it any longer as a geopolitical insurance policy for weaker states. However, they advance an affirmative argument: investment arbitration, they assert, boosts economic growth. This proposition has a more convincing ring to it than the self-defence theory. When a state consents to investment arbitration, it offers foreign investors an effective legal procedure. Investors no longer have to worry about the reliability of local courts. Because investment arbitration protects foreign investors in that way, so the argument goes, the government that offers to arbitrate will attract more foreign investment. Note that two empirical assertions are necessary for the argument to work: provide investment arbitration, because investment arbitration attracts foreign investors; attract foreign investors, because foreign investors boost the economy.

Whatever its benefits, agreeing to investment arbitration carries costs. It takes power away from domestic dispute settlement organs, including the courts. And it imposes substantive rules that might conflict with public policy priorities. Whether to bear these costs is a political decision involving value judgments that are for each society to make. But it is hard for a society to reach a reasoned decision about a cost–benefit relationship if nobody knows how to quantify the cost or the benefit. What is more, going back to the empirical assertions behind the pro-arbitration argument, recent studies have struggled to find convincing evidence to support them.

Does investment arbitration attract investment?

When companies consider whether to invest, evidence suggests that the availability of investment arbitration has practically nothing to do with it. In-house lawyers of large US companies, when asked, said so flat out: they barely ever see the presence of investment treaties as a relevant consideration when deciding whether to green-light an investment project—even though it is precisely their job to be their company's anxious bodyguard.

Field data suggest the same conclusion. Take France's BITs (bilateral investment treaties) as an example. The French government over the years has signed more than a hundred BITs. Researchers have not found that France's BITs correlate to any increase in investments by French companies in the other countries that are parties to those BITs. What makes French investors want to invest in a given country seems to be something other than the legal protection offered by a BIT. So, if French investors are representative of EU investors as a whole, there would seem to be no reason grounded in data for a country entering a BIT with the EU to expect an investment windfall either.

France is just one example. Studies covering other parts of the world, and investment flows globally, come to similar conclusions. There is little, if any, evidence that signing investment treaties containing arbitration clauses brings a country more foreign investment.

And even when a country does receive more foreign investment, it does not necessarily benefit the country's economy. The evidence linking foreign investments and economic growth is in fact surprisingly weak. The hypothesis that investment arbitration brings advantages to the host state fails repeatedly to find validation in the data: arbitration does not seem to foster investment; and investment does not necessarily foster growth.

These empirical results puzzle many experts. It has not been clearly established why increased access to the rule of law, made possible by the option to use investment arbitration, would not be a meaningful factor in companies' investment strategies. Undoubtedly certain kinds of investors care more than others about the existence of reliable institutions. Ongoing research indeed explores the idea that only investors accustomed to reliable institutions and a high level of rule of law in their home country look for the same thing abroad. French investors and American lawyers both come from rule of law cultures however. Neither seem much to care about the availability of investment arbitration.

States rarely if ever talk about their investment treaties as evidence that they are a good place to invest. Favourable tax policies, skilled labour, good infrastructure—these are things that states talk about in promotional campaigns, but pro-arbitration treaty clauses, not so much. The rationale might be similar to that of an aspiring tourist island that boasts about its sunshine, sandy beaches, and luxurious hotels—not its state-of-the-art malaria clinics and its recent successes against the guerrillas. Boasting about treaty protections that guard against government abuse attracts attention to the abuse, not to the protections.

Another factor that might explain the rather weak impact of investment treaties on investment decisions is that businesspeople often focus more on the substance of a project or transaction than on the legal procedures they will use if something goes wrong. Such selective focus is not unique to businesses making an overseas investment. When companies negotiate any sort of contract, the dispute resolution clause is typically dealt with quickly at the eleventh hour (much to the chagrin of lawyers). Consider, for instance, that Japanese investors are among those who invest the most abroad (in 2018 Japan had the world's largest investment outflow), yet they have only ever filed three publicly known investment arbitrations. It is not likely that this is because Japanese investors virtually never run into trouble with a government abroad. More likely, they have found ways to resolve their disputes that do not involve fighting it out in arbitration. Tolerance for adversary proceedings varies across different businesses and across business cultures; but it is probably a universal tendency to hope that, somehow, one's business will get through without an irreparable breakdown, whether with business partners or with governments. That may well be another reason that the availability of arbitration has had less influence on investment decisions than arbitration's champions assert.

The price to pay for the rule of law

So perhaps consenting to investment arbitration does not bring the consenting state economic growth, perhaps not even any real increase in foreign investments. But one may think of more abstract benefits, such as advancing the rule of law. It is natural, for us in the 21st century, to think that there must be some good in more international law, more international law enforcement, more international tribunals, more legal remedies for aggrieved parties.

The problem with abstract benefits like advancing the rule of law is that they have concrete, quantifiable downsides. Consider in this regard, for instance, the co-called reputational effect of investment arbitration claims. Once a state is hit by an investment arbitration claim—just a notice of arbitration being filed, in order to initiate arbitration proceedings—foreign investments to that country tend to diminish. In short, the claim itself damages the reputation of the state, and potential investors take flight. The evidence, as we have seen, does not show that arbitration attracts investment, but rather that arbitration can scare investment away when the state has provoked a claim against it. In this regard at least, investment arbitration is not symmetric in its benefits and costs.

And it gets worse. Investment claims have this negative reputational effect regardless of the legal strength of the claim. A chill settles on investment even when the investment claim is almost completely frivolous. This is not surprising: the precise merits of a claim are hard for other investors to assess confidently or quickly. Moreover, investors begin to flee the moment a claim is brought, and it may take several years for a tribunal to dismiss a frivolous one. Thanks to investment arbitration, individual investors in effect hold the host country hostage to this extent. True, it is not cost-free for an investor to use arbitration—credibly filing a claim is likely to cost several hundred thousand dollars in legal fees, and a lot more to move it forward through the proceedings. But the cost on the state is likely to be much more, due to the impact on its reputation. Investors, then, can use the threat of arbitration to bargain states into settlements that the states otherwise would reject. Empirical research suggests that tobacco companies, for example, have used the threat of investment arbitration to extract substantial concessions from governments.

We have focused here on investment chill, which is a concern mostly among less developed states. There is also the possibility that arbitration puts a chill on regulatory and legislative measures, including in the most developed states. The higher the cost of a proposed law or regulation, the less likely a legislature or administrative agency will adopt it. Even rules already on the books are affected, because governments are always making tough choices about where to focus executive and prosecutorial resources: the threat of arbitration might lead governments to leave some rules unenforced. Whether to curb smoking, protect the environment, or mitigate a pandemic, adopting and enforcing regulations is costly. Investment arbitration may increase the cost.

It also may tip the cost–benefit analysis against adopting new regulations or enforcing those a country already has. This has had visible effects on public policy in Canada for example—one of the developed states that have most often been respondents in investment arbitrations. The province of Ontario abandoned a number of environmental initiatives because they risked provoking investors to arbitrate. Political scientists aptly call this 'regulatory chill': regulations would have been passed had it not been for investment arbitration. Representatives from the Trade Ministry buried regulatory proposals in inter-ministerial processes by invoking the risk of investment arbitration. This happened mostly while the proposals were still in the hands of government lawyers and bureaucrats, before political representatives even had a chance to consider them. Critics of investment arbitration complain that an arcane technocratic institution rooted in international treaties has come to bypass representative democracy. A business executive or investment lawyer might in turn dismiss the critics as populist rabble. But the questions that investment arbitration poses are real.

What rule of law?

Romans used to say *dura lex sed lex*. The law is tough, but the law it is. If that maxim were the only guide, then one might ask what all the fuss over arbitration is about. Countries consent to arbitration of claims by investors that their rights have been violated, including rights that would be violated by any number of actions that the country might like to take. If competing social interests demand regulatory action, then a government remains free to regulate; it simply has to compensate investors if the new regulation violates their rights. From that point of view, it is not arbitrators' fault if the government's social agenda now costs more to implement; that is the predictable result of a commitment that the country freely entered into. The government should have considered the trade-offs involved before it committed to investment arbitration. The investment treaty might be tough law, but its requirements should not surprise the state that adopts it. Or so the defenders of investment arbitration would say.

Governments, however, often have not thought much at all about the trade-offs when they adopt an investment treaty containing an arbitration clause. In many instances, in particular in developing countries, diplomats have signed such treaties not because careful consideration recommended it. They have signed the treaties instead as a matter of workaday diplomacy, as a sign of friendship between countries, as a symbol of collaboration with other states. These are mostly fairly short treaties, their substantive provisions often cookie-cutter templates, usually proposed by the richer state in the negotiation. A country does not even need to bring a drafting expert to the negotiations. The treaty comes as-is, ready to sign. For a government keen to show that it is a good international citizen, for a prime minister travelling abroad to showcase her country on a larger stage, negotiating a BIT looks like a perfect public relations move. Everybody wants more investment. It is awkward to object to a treaty with a title such as 'Treaty for the Promotion and Protection of Reciprocal Trade and Investment'.

In a number of cases, the reason for signing BITs was even more mundane. A study by Lauge Poulsen of University College London and Emma Aisbett of the Australian National University revealed that a number of diplomats, particularly in developing countries, having to justify their salary and expensive international travels, considered that the best way to do so was by drawing attention to the number of treaties they signed. Among the different types of treaties, those dealing with investments seemed to be among the easiest to conclude.

Yet, under both the law of treaties and the unwritten rules of international relations, it is assumed that a state knows what it is doing when it freely enters into a treaty. A treaty binds the state; a change of government or change of heart does not cancel a state's existing treaties. The whole of society, however, not just the leaders who signed them, may end up paying the price that a treaty imposes.

When one invokes the 'tough law' maxim, this suggests that the law is a machine, its cogs and wheels, once set in motion, automatic in their result. In legal philosophy, this is sometimes called legal formalism: the formal logic of law, like that of mathematics, applies to any given fact problem and, properly applied, gives a correct result. But it is not the only way to look at the law. An important reason that cogs-and-wheels cannot be the only way to think about the law is that law has its ambiguities; there would not be legal disputes if it did not. Investment law is no exception in this regard.

BITs give investors legal rights, but the BITs express these rights in very general terms. The correct way to interpret and apply the terms of a BIT is therefore by no means self-evident. To give the main examples, investment treaties typically promise investors the following:

(a) No expropriation, direct or indirect, without adequate compensation;
(b) Fair and equitable treatment;
(c) Due process;
(d) No discrimination or arbitrary treatment.

A broad cross-section of lawyers, investors, and ordinary citizens would readily agree that particular, obvious examples of misconduct are violations of terms such as these. If a state were to declare that all Swiss investors (but only Swiss investors) are a public enemy and then proceeded to seize all Swiss investors' assets without any court hearing, then this would be a violation. Once one moves away from such an extreme scenario, however, agreeing to an interpretation is not easy.

One might expect arbitral decisions to hover around some middle ground when arbitrators interpret and apply treaty protections to states in close cases. Over time, however, as decisions of arbitral tribunals have accumulated, the treaty protections have tended to expand. This is due to the interpretations reached by arbitrators, even as every good arbitrator strives to explain her interpretations as springing naturally from the legal text. As the protections have expanded, the obligations on states have become more onerous.

Today the same legal provisions, expressing the same nominal legal rights, typically protect investors a great deal more than they did twenty years ago. Fair and equitable treatment, for instance, arguably requires much more of states, and protects investors much more, than it did when many of the investment treaties were signed. If more investor protection means higher costs for competing public policies, and if higher costs for such policies mean *dura lex*—tough law—then arbitral tribunals have indeed made the law tougher. Few if any states, when they accepted the investment treaties in the first place, bargained for an ongoing evolution of the law that has mostly been in favour of the foreign investor.

Quirks in the system

All these complaints aside, one might assume that investment arbitration at least leads to more predictable results than disparate national courts, to fairer results than prejudiced local judges, and to well-reasoned decisions that states can use as a guide to improve their own legal systems. That was the dream of the progenitors of modern arbitration at Paris in 1919, after all: an overarching, global rule of law, bringing justice irrespective of nation or creed. But has arbitration lived up to such expectations?

In at least some respects, it has not. Most strikingly, investment arbitration has not produced outcomes that lawyers can reliably predict on the basis of a principled analysis of the law and the facts in a case. In respect of a range of questions, substantive and procedural, investment tribunals have produced totally disparate results. What is the definition of 'investment'? It depends on which tribunal you ask. Which regulatory measures constitute an unlawful expropriation? Again, it depends on the arbitrators. To what extent may an investment tribunal apply a garden-variety commercial contract? What does a 'most-favoured nation' clause mean? When does an investor hold the nationality required to obtain protection under the treaty? When taking steps that impose burdens upon an investor, under what conditions may a state plead necessity (as many states have in emergencies, and as many more almost surely will in the wake of the COVID-19 pandemic)? Does 'fair and equitable' denote a general international law requirement, identical in all situations, or does it arise specially out of particular investment treaties? To each of these questions, different tribunals have given different, and in many instances irreconcilable, answers. It is far from clear that investment tribunals behave more predictably than national courts. The best predictor of an investment arbitration, it is often said in the field, is who has been appointed arbitrator.

There is also a suspicion that investment arbitrators are business-biased—that they favour investors and private interests over states and public interests. Why they might be biased is established. For one thing, most investment arbitrators work in law firms. Law firms on average make more money (a lot more) advising investors than they make advising states. Second, an arbitration needs to be started, if an arbitrator is to be appointed. Who decides to start an arbitration? The claimants. Who are the claimants? Investors. Arbitrators have an economic incentive to make it easy for investors to file claims, for it is those claims that create demand for arbitrators' services. Notice that the incentive is aligned very differently for standing, permanent courts: once the judges of a court have their hands full, they have an incentive to make it *difficult* to lodge a claim. Arbitrators do not belong to any single curial body with an interest in keeping a lid on its caseload. On the contrary, the number of investment arbitrators sharing the work has virtually no limit, because they are appointed on a case-by-case basis, and there are far more lawyers who might serve as arbitrators than there is any foreseeable need for arbitration.

Researchers, concerned with the possibility that states suffer from an unfair bias in arbitration, have considered empirical evidence, but the evidence is open to more than one interpretation. The first thing one notices is that investors win in only 35–45 per cent of the cases, states in 55–65 per cent. All else being equal, this data would suggest that *investors* suffer from bias in arbitration, not states. However, a simple win–loss ratio in itself does not tell us whether the process is unfair or to whom. As we have noted, arbitrators have an incentive to encourage claims; the incentive runs the same way for the law firms that work for investors. Such an alignment of incentives is not conducive to a rigorous and selective approach to claims. On the contrary, it encourages claims, including claims that arguably ought not to be brought at all. A deep, qualitative analysis of claims would be needed to form a judgment on whether the observed win–loss ratio comports with expectations of fairness. It is a possibility at least worth considering that, if the claims that ought never to have been brought, claims that were at best extreme long-shots, are not counted, then the results favour investors.

Another concern is with the quality of the decisions that investment arbitrators hand down. An investment arbitrator typically is paid from US $200,000 to US $1,000,000 per case. At such fees, one expects better than 'egregious errors in the reasoning' and reasoning that is 'practically non-existent', as Federico Ortino of King's College London describes a series of decisions. One certainly should expect—indeed, demand—absolutely sterling ethics, beyond even the appearance of conflict of interest. And, yet, investment arbitration, for all its lack of a single, centralized managerial organ, and for all the divergent interpretations it has produced of the legal provisions it applies, is a surprisingly closely held profession. By 2012, just fifteen arbitrators had handled 55 per cent of all investment cases and 75 per cent of the cases over US $4 billion.

Reactions

Investment arbitration is power. Arbitral tribunals can, and do, order governments to pay billions of dollars in compensation to foreign companies. Even when these governments have acted in ways that are for the public good, for example, in trying to protect the environment or public health. Even when these governments were in the midst of financial collapse. Investment arbitration has the power to increase the costs of policies that are at odds with the interests of foreign companies. It has the power to harm the reputation of states and drain the public purse. And of every exercise of power we must ask: Why?

The 'why' for the investors is easy to answer. The exercising of the power to arbitrate investors' claims against states potentially delivers enormous benefits to the investor who can convince a panel of party-appointed arbitrators that the state is in breach of an obligation. Winning claims have delivered billions to the investors who make them. As we have suggested above, however, the 'why' for the states is not so clear.

Yet states have been muted in their protests, to the extent that they have protested at all. True, when Bolivia, Ecuador, and Venezuela quit the ICSID Convention (the main multilateral framework for investment arbitration) in the late 2000s and early 2010s, it looked like they were starting a trend. The chain reaction that some observers predicted, however, did not come to pass. Though even the World Economic Forum in Davos now says that preserving 'adequate policy space' is a challenge that investment arbitration needs to address, a current study by Yoram Haftel of the Hebrew University of Jerusalem and Alexander Thompson of Ohio State University shows that 'states have not made a systematic effort... to recalibrate their BITs for the purpose of preserving more regulatory space. In fact, most renegotiations either leave [investment arbitration] provisions unchanged or render them more investor-friendly.'

So, if investment arbitration is such a bad deal for states, why do they continue to accept it? For one thing, the drawbacks mentioned above are generalizations across the whole range of experience with arbitration. States do not set policy on the basis of such generalizations. They do so on the basis of their specific circumstances. Certain states may have thoroughly studied the advantages and drawbacks of consenting to investment arbitration in their particular circumstances and have concluded that they are an exception, that, for them, investment arbitration is a good deal.

Second, the description once favoured by some international relations theorists of states as billiard balls—objects that interact with one another but whose internal make-up does not affect their interaction—is not adequate. States have complex inner workings. Any given international policy that a state pursues is not necessarily supported by all the interests in the country or in its government. Different ministries typically pursue different objectives. Investment treaties are likely to be pet projects of trade ministries. Even when the environment ministry or labour ministry starts to feel uneasy, this might not overcome the inertia favouring continued respect for treaties already adopted.

Third, states often really appreciate the risk of being hit by an investment arbitration only once it actually occurs: the prospect of facing an investor's claim does not focus the policy-makers' imagination as much as the reality of a claim that they now face. By the time an investor has made a claim, however, it is too late for the state to back out of the commitment to arbitrate.

Investment arbitration is still a relatively new institution. More than half the investment claims ever filed have been filed in the period since 2010. Some claims take years to reach a final award. So the flow of information about arbitration is slow and changing. It might be that states are only starting to realize the full impact of the experiment that they have committed to.

If a state announces its intention to withdraw from its arbitration commitments, then under typical treaty terms it may be some months or a year before those commitments end. Arbitrations already under way continue. Depending on how the arbitration clause is written (and which arbitrators interpret it), an investor might be able to institute arbitration after the state has expressed its intention to quit the treaty. Under some interpretations of some treaty regimes, claims can even be received after the state has completed its withdrawal if the facts behind the claims arose beforehand—that is, the possibility of bringing a claim could, at least for a period, outlive the treaty. As for renegotiating a treaty, this requires that both parties reach consensus on new terms, a difficult thing to achieve and seldom achieved quickly. As for ignoring a treaty obligation, this can entail considerable costs, especially for smaller states.

It is possible, even likely, that a further wave of anti-arbitration sentiment is coming. We mentioned above the concerns over the dispute settlement provisions in TTIP and the reduction of

8. 'No thanks to parallel justice': a growing wave of anti-arbitration.

arbitration options in the USMCA. Parties involved in those developments—France, Germany, the US—are among the most advanced economies of the world. If a renewed backlash against investment arbitration comes, then it might well come from the developed states too, not just from a handful of less developed, capital-importing states. And, as Figure 8 suggests, the anti-arbitration sentiment is no longer the preserve of specialists; it has spread to parts of the wider public.

Fourth, reliable information about the wider implications of investment arbitration for society, based on methodologically sound, replicated empirical studies, has not been available for very long. It was not until 2010 that a major book was published, edited by Michael Waibel, then of the University of Cambridge, and several colleagues, which first took a critical look at investment arbitration as a system. Almost all the work on the topic before then was by lawyers who serve as arbitrators or as counsel in arbitrations or both, or by academic experts who were concerned chiefly with the technical legal aspects of arbitration.

The approach from such insiders had been to work on solutions within the system, not to critique the system as a whole or to ask how it affects the interests of the constituencies whom it is supposed to serve.

The rise of serious scholarship that looks at investment arbitration in the round has been slowed, in part, by the response of the insiders. As David Schneiderman of the University of Toronto recently put it, investment 'lawyers and arbitrators are manning the barricades' in the battle against all those who 'put...into doubt the merits of the legal regime'; the doubters are not interlocutors to be reasoned with, but 'enemies to be vanquished'. True, one expects practitioners in any speciality to defend their turf. And let us be fair: this is not like the tobacco industry that once told us that smoking might actually be healthy.

And yet the concerns to which investment arbitration gives rise are not to be set aside lightly, and the need for a balanced assessment is real. In 2012 two whistle-blowers pointed out an important difference between the old debate over smoking and the new one over investment arbitration. Oncologists and cancer researchers were not in the business of selling cigarettes, and so they had no predisposition to side with the tobacco industry. The experts whom we might ask to evaluate investment arbitration, by contrast, are almost entirely the same people who *are* in the business of 'selling' investment arbitration. The investment lawyers tell investors that they had best escape the stacked deck of biased, local courts. Meanwhile, in the growing public debate over investment arbitration, the investment lawyers, so far, have been judge, jury, and star witness. Other views are starting to influence the politics behind investment arbitration. How far this goes remains to be seen.

Chapter 6
Where is arbitration going?

Has it been a good idea to privatize justice?

For a long time, few people even posed the question. Arbitration was below the radar, a specialist discipline attracting little general interest, much less public concern. But arbitration has emerged from obscurity. Once a tool of commercial traders who sought quick and efficient settlement when deals went wrong, arbitration now covers an expansive variety of relationships. Settling a truly private matter by privatized justice when both parties truly consent is unobjectionable. The provocation comes from the prolific application of arbitration across the world to cases where there are sharp disparities in the bargaining power of the parties or where the arbitral outcome inevitably affects the public interest and community values.

Judges are public servants, on public payroll, lodged within public systems of review, appeal, and control. Litigants do not tell the judges how broad, or how narrow, the judges' jurisdiction is or how to run their court rooms. Judges do not depend upon the litigants for their jobs. With arbitrators, it is the other way around. Arbitrators may be justice-givers, like judges, but they are private actors. They are not subject to any constraining specific code of practice and may not even be subject to the usual codes of practice of lawyers, as arbitrators do not in principle have to be members of any bar. And, as private actors, arbitrators work only when, and to the extent, parties have consented to them deciding a dispute. In arbitration, parties call the shots, or at least some parties do.

The privatization of justice through arbitration no doubt has advantages. It has thrived, and rational actors are using it. Arbitrators are out of work the moment they deliver a final award in the case, and they have a professional, and financial, interest in getting appointed by future parties in future disputes. So, if you are the one who pays the arbitrators, you can count on the arbitrators paying heed to what you say. You are not looking for grandiose gestures towards public law or obsessions over the systematic development of the jurisprudence. Just a healthy, party-centred focus on applying a stipulated set of substantive rules, under a stipulated procedure, for purposes of dealing with *your* dispute and your dispute only. It is these very advantages of arbitration, however, that now provoke public concern. Privatized justice all too readily looks like justice for hire.

This is the perception setting off alarm bells, and not just among academics whom businesspeople and arbitration lawyers sometimes dismiss as standing in the way of those in the 'real world' who prefer doing rather than talking. The bells are now ringing in many circles, even if the arbitration industry itself tries to project confidence that all is well.

At least two distinct problems associated with justice for hire—if that is what arbitration really is—have triggered concern.

First, in some disputes that go to arbitration, it is really only *one* party who has made a meaningful decision to arbitrate. Where that is the case, then it may be that only *that* party has a meaningful say in the choice of their justice-giver. This is a problem that some say arises when large companies include arbitration clauses in contracts they enter with consumers. (See Box 5.)

**Box 5 A coming dark age for dispute settlement?
A judge's warning**

Employers, Internet service providers, and consumer lenders
have led a mass exodus from the court system. By the click of a
mouse or tick of a box, the American public is constantly
inveigled to divert the enforcement of its legal rights to venues
closed off from public scrutiny. Justice is becoming privatized,
like so many other formerly public goods turned over to invisible
hands—electricity, water, education, prisons, highways, the
military.

Source: Judge Stephen Wm. Smith, 'Are US Courts Going Dark?', *Just Security* 6
May 2016.

Consent is always a formal requirement for arbitration. But is
consent always free in fact as well as form? Asymmetries in
bargaining position exist in practically all relationships, but some
are extreme. (See Figure 9.) Arbitration started as a private
initiative to provide business actors with reliable rules when
public institutions were faltering or too slow. Now, however, the
media describe arbitration as a 'far-reaching power play
orchestrated by...corporations' that 'effectively forced millions of
people to sign away their rights to go to court', barring them from
accessing 'the only tool citizens have to fight illegal or deceitful
business practices'—that being the *New York Times*'s view. *The
Economist*, by no means a tribune of radical opinion, for its part
concludes that 'the implementation of this laudable idea has been
disastrous'. To some who now encounter arbitration, it evokes the
worst excesses of laissez-faire: private courts in a dystopian world
designed for the convenience of the powerful few at the expense of
everyone else.

The second problem is that, even if more or less equal parties give
the go-ahead to arbitration—say, two large companies each

I desperately want this job.

Good, because we desperately want you to sign this arbitration agreement.

stus.com

9. When consent to arbitration is not free.

equipped with world-class lawyers—their disputes, though private in form, might be public in effect. The larger the dispute, the more likely it has some impact that goes beyond the parties to the dispute. Did the early exponents of arbitration, such as the Merchants of Peace who met in Paris in 1919, think that arbitration would be a tool for self-dealing in the hands of crony capitalists looking to dip into the public purse? Did the drafters of ICSID, mindful of the balance between the rights of investors and host governments, think that arbitrators might deter or punish governments from taking emergency health measures in a pandemic? Such people no doubt would be pleased that arbitration has grown and spread to the extent it has. Whether they would be pleased with all its effects is less certain.

So, when we look at the big picture, is privatized justice to be promoted, or should it be restrained? What should the verdict be on arbitration?

A fair reply is, *it depends*. To ask whether arbitration is good or bad is like asking whether austerity measures are good or bad, whether privatization helps or hurts, whether taxes should be high or low. Protagonists in the respective debates proffer arguments both ways. The debate over arbitration, as with so many others, tends to get lost in a jumble of facts, interests, political views, and knee-jerk reactions. Clear answers have been elusive.

And the answers one gives in the debate over arbitration, as in so many debates over institutions that affect the public interest, are often shaped by one's ideological starting point. The US Supreme Court has split along party lines when asked to say how far the Federal Arbitration Act goes to require courts to refuse arbitration of employment disputes. In a case applying the Act in 2018, the pro-arbitration majority were Republican appointees; all four dissenters were appointed by Democrats. An essentialist approach hardly explains all the vagaries of arbitration—but it would miss part of the picture to ignore that an ideological component exists.

The battle lines have not been static. Before legislatures stepped in, courts in many countries were outright hostile to arbitration, and without distinction as to who was arbitrating against whom over what. Today, it is far more often law academics who vilify arbitration than the courts. Earlier, this was not the case. Recall the heady mood that we described at the beginning of this book. Arbitration had its roots in an idealistic vision. Its exponents proclaimed that a new, consent-based system would revolutionize dispute settlement, foster peace among nations, build a new world.

In recent years, the paradigm has shifted. The shift is most pronounced with respect to investment arbitration. The new core belief in the field is that arbitration, for lack of a better word, is *bad*. Book proposals to university presses and article submissions to the more high-minded periodicals now mostly join the anti-arbitration chorus. Professors, if they say something complimentary about arbitration, and especially investment arbitration, come under sharp critique from their students.

Candidates for academic posts are crossed off lists because of their professional association with law firms that represent investors in arbitrations against governments. Students hector their classmates who articulate a pro-arbitration argument.

What, then, is to become of arbitration in the years ahead? A reasonable way forward may be to go back to where we began. Businesses developed arbitration to get their disputes out of the way in a fair and expeditious manner. Arbitration was not meant to simulate an alternate legal reality that swallows unwilling or unwitting parties with no hope of escape. Nor was it envisaged that parallel arbitration universes would eclipse the institutions that modern societies have entrusted with their most serious collective questions. 'Back to basics' is not a complete answer, but it might provide some needed inspiration.

In arbitration, *compétence-compétence* is a key technical term, because it denotes a power of the arbitrator that, if exercised correctly, assures that arbitration works as intended. This is the power that arbitrators exercise to identify the lines between what they are to decide and what they are not to. Arbitrators need this power if they are to function. But the wider legal system has its necessary powers, too. Among these is the power to identify lines between the private and the public, lines separating those questions that citizens may regulate *inter partes* and those which society at large has a valid claim to address. It would be an exorbitant overreach, and a confusion of categories, if arbitrators thought their competence went so far as to identify *those* lines themselves. Arbitration is in many respects a self-contained regime, policing its own affairs; but it is not for arbitration alone to say where it belongs in the larger legal, political, and societal frame. Arbitration is not an institution equipped to decide what our collective values are. Arbitrators and the parties who call upon them will remain conscious of both its promise and its limits, if they mean this noble institution well.

References

Chapter 1: What is arbitration and where does it come from?

Alabama arbitration as a turning point in the history of arbitration:
    Adrian Cook, *The Alabama Claims* (Cornell University Press 1975).
'an indemnity of US $15,500,000 in gold': Roy Jenkins, *Gladstone*
    (Macmillan 1995), p. 359.
'"an act of sovereignty of the Iranian nation is not referable to
    arbitration"': Minister of Finance of Iran to the Anglo-Iranian Oil
    Company, *Anglo-Iranian Oil case*, ICJ 1951, vol. III, pp. 693–4.
'whether they were in touch with the US government about a
    military intervention': House of Commons Debate, 29 May 1951,
    vol. 488 c. 43.
'arbitrators appear to imitate the judges with whom they are most
    familiar': Thomas Schultz, 'The Arbitration Ethos', in Thomas
    Schultz and Federico Ortino (eds), *The Oxford Handbook of
    International Arbitration* (Oxford University Press 2020).
'arbitrators are typically lawyers who specialize in arbitration': Thomas
    Schultz and Robert Kovacs, 'The Rise of a Third Generation of
    Arbitrators? Fifteen Years after Dezalay & Garth', *Arbitration
    International* 28 (2012): 163.

Chapter 2: How arbitration works

'The UN's International Law Commission (the ILC) in 1949 chose
    arbitral procedure': Model Rules on Arbitral Procedure 1958,
    ILC Yearbook 1958, vol. II, pp. 83–6.

'model arbitration clauses published by the London Court of International Arbitration': https://www.lcia.org/Dispute_ Resolution_Services/LCIA_Recommended_Clauses.aspx

'Appointment provisions...American Arbitration Association proposes': American Arbitration Association, *Drafting Dispute Resolution Clauses: A Practical Guide* (2013).

'an example...of the operative part of an award': Final Award in ICC case no. 11307 of 2003 (*Corp. X* v. *Corp. Y*).

'an example of the operative part of an award in an investment case': *Cortec Mining Kenya Ltd* v. *Kenya*, ICSID Case No. ARB/15/29 (Award) (Binnie, President; Dharmananda & Stern, Members), 22 October 2018, p. 405.

'contain permanent mechanisms for carrying out a limited review of awards': https://iccwbo.org/publication/arbitration-rules-and-mediation-rules/

'a watchful eye on how national courts treat arbitration awards': see, for example, Koki Yanagisawa and Takiko Kadono, 'Setting Aside Arbitral Awards before Japanese Courts: Consolidating Japan's Position as an Arbitration-Friendly Jurisdiction?' Kluwer Arbitration Blog (22 January 2018); Sadaff Habib, 'Spotlight on Ethiopia as it Annuls a Euro 20 million Arbitral Award', Kluwer Arbitration Blog (14 August 2018).

Chapter 3: The multiple lives of arbitration

'at least 300 times as many commercial disputes go to court as go to arbitration': Michael Reynolds, *An Overview of the Use of Arbitration in England*, Oxford Centre For Socio-Legal Studies Research Paper (2014), referring to Mark Ramseyer and Eric B. Rasmusen, *Comparative Litigation Rates*, Harvard John M. Olin Discussion Paper Series, No. 681, November 2010. See also Markus Altenkirch and Jan Frohloff, 'International Arbitration Statistics 2016—Busy Times for Arbitral Institutions', *Global Arbitration Review*, 26 June 2017.

'some say it denies consumers a fair hearing in court': in the US, arbitration prevents class actions in court (lawsuits filed collectively by people who are in the same situation), which, because they are collective, decrease the costs of access to justice. Some believe, on the other hand, that arbitration can be better than class actions: see, from the US Chamber of Commerce, David Hirschmann and Lisa Rickard, 'Why we need to save arbitration. The CFPB says its new rule will help consumers. But all it will do is enrich trial lawyers', *Politico*, 5 May 2016.

'the *New York Times*...published a series of scathing articles in 2015 about the supposed evils of consumer arbitration': Jessica Silver-Greenberg and Robert Gebeloff, 'Beware the Fine Print, Part I: Arbitration Everywhere, Stacking the Deck of Justice', *The New York Times*, 31 October 2015; Jessica Silver-Greenberg and Michael Corkery, 'Beware the Fine Print, Part II: In Arbitration, a "Privatization of the Justice System"', *The New York Times*, 1 November 2015; Jessica Silver-Greenberg and Michael Corkery, 'Beware the Fine Print, Part III: Arbitration Everywhere, Stacking the Deck of Justice', *The New York Times*, 2 November 2015.

'most prominent arbitration institutions': the overwhelming majority of arbitrations administered by the London Court of International Arbitration are seated in London: in 2018, out of 285 new arbitrations, 218 were seated in the United Kingdom. Arbitrations administered by the International Chamber of Commerce, during the 1995–2012 period, had their seats in the following cities (according to Gary B. Born, *International Commercial Arbitration* (2nd edn) (Kluwer Law International 2014): France: 1478 (24%), Switzerland: 1451 (23%), UK: 885, US: 609, Germany: 365, Singapore: 280. Beyond the LCIA and the ICC; all arbitrations registered by the Hong Kong International Arbitration Centre in 2017 were seated in Hong Kong, 73 per cent of the cases commenced in 2017 before the Stockholm Chamber of Commerce were seated in Stockholm, and in 2018, the German Arbitration Institute registered 118 new cases seated in Germany. According to a survey conducted by Queen Mary University of London and the law firm White & Case, the preferred places for arbitration are London and Paris, followed by Singapore, Hong Kong, and Geneva (Queen Mary & White & Case (2018), *2018 International Arbitration Survey: The Evolution of International Arbitration*, p. 9.)

'French energy giant EDF...diplomatic protection': see Prezzo Luce, 'Nucleare in Italia: il famoso accordo tra Enel e EDF', https://prezzoluce.it/attori/accordo-enel-edf

'case of Bernard Tapie': this was widely reported in the French media, as well as in specialized arbitration publications. Relevant articles include Etienne Jacbo, 'Arbitrage Tapie: le grand récit d'une affaire tentaculaire', *Le Figaro*, 11 March 2019; Alicia Paulet, 'Affaire Tapie: 25 ans d'imbroglio judiciaire', *Le Figaro*, 30 October 2017;

Jehan-Damien Le Brusq, *The Tapie Saga: Paris Successfully Passed the Test*, Kluwer Arbitration Blog, 1 September 2016. His life is chronicled in Marie-Adelaïde Scigacz and Kocila Makdeche, 'Bernard Tapie: le grand jeu de sa vie', *FranceInfo*. On Christine Lagarde's role, see for instance 'Guilty Verdict for I.M.F. Chief Christine Lagarde: A Primer', *The New York Times*, 19 December 2016.

'"justice bubble for the privileged"': Anil Yilmaz Vastardis, 'Investment Treaty Arbitration: A Justice Bubble for the Privileged' in Thomas Schultz and Federico Ortino (eds), *The Oxford Handbook of International Arbitration* (Oxford University Press 2020).

Chapter 4: Arbitration and the law

'Legislatures began adopting laws to support arbitration': Yves Dezalay and Bryant G. Garth, 'International Commercial Arbitration: The Creation of a Legal Market' in Thomas Schultz and Federico Ortino (eds), *The Oxford Handbook of International Arbitration* (Oxford University Press 2020).

'US Supreme Court said in 2019, a "private agreement may be crystal clear and require arbitration"': *New Prime Inc.* v. *Oliveira*, 139 S.Ct., pp. 532, 537–8 (Gorsuch, J. 2019).

'States traditionally have also been cautious about letting arbitrators decide matters of family law': see Wendy Kennett, 'It's Arbitration, but Not as We Know It: Reflections on Family Law Dispute Resolution', *International Journal of Law, Policy and the Family* 30 (2016): 1; and Institute of Family Law Arbitrators, *A Guide to the Family Law Arbitration Scheme* (3rd edn), last accessed December 2019.

'company asked a US court to order India…to allow the company back into India's maritime area': *Hardy Exploration & Production (India), Inc.* v. *Government of India*, Ministry of Petroleum & Natural Gas, US D. Ct., DC (7 June 2018).

'a court in the US…order Russia to return certain texts and artefacts': *Chabad* v. *Russian Federation*, 915 F. Supp. 2d 148, 150–2 (D.D.C. 2013).

'a US court ordered Venezuela to respect an arbitral award indicating specific performance of…a hotel': *Four Seasons Hotels & Resorts, B.V.* v. *Consorcio Barr, S.A.*, 613 F.Supp. 2d 1362, 1369 (S.D. Florida 2009).

'"there exists a general principle of law...that contracts which seriously violate *bonos mores* or international public policy"': Lagergren's award: ICC Case No. 1110 (1963).

'contract between Iraq and an armaments company for sale of military helicopters': *Governo e Ministeri della Repubblica dell'Iraq* v. *Armamenti e Aerospazio S.p.A., et al* (22 September 2015).

'Arbitration and money laundering' (Box 4): already in 2002, the International Chamber of Commerce Institute of World Business Law held an international conference on 'Arbitration—Money Laundering, Corruption and Fraud' (proceedings published in Kristine Karsten and Andrew Berkeley (eds), *Arbitration: Money Laundering, Corruption and Fraud* (Kluwer Law International 2006). More recently, see Patricia Nacimiento, Tilmann Hertel, and Catrice Gayer, *Arbitration and Money Laundering: What Are the Obligations Placed on Counsel and Arbitrators and What Risks Do They Face?* Kluwer Arbitration Blog, 10 November 2017; Competence Centre Arbitration and Crime, Basel Institute on Governance, University of Basel, *Corruption and Money Laundering in International Arbitration: A Toolkit for Arbitrators*, April 2019.

Chapter 5: The politics of arbitration against governments

'"Justice...manifestly and undoubtedly seen to be done"': Lord Chief Justice Hewart in *R* v. *Sussex Justices, Ex parte McCarthy* [1924] 1 KB 256, [1923] All ER Rep 233.

'arbitrations and a "backlash"': Michael Waibel et al. (eds), *The Backlash against Investment Arbitration: Perceptions and Reality* (Kluwer Law International 2010).

'*The Economist* and *Financial Times*...raised questions about investment arbitration': Terra Lawson-Remer, 'Investor-State Dispute Settlement: The Arbitration Game', *The Economist*, 11 October 2014; John Kay, 'Free Trade Should Not Put Democracy in the Dock', *The Financial Times*, 4 February 2015.

'"most toxic acronym in Europe"': Paul Ames, 'ISDS: The Most Toxic Acronym in Europe', *Politico EU*, 17 September 2015.

'The Cato Institute...questioning the benefits of investment arbitration': Cato Institute Policy Analysis 'Liberalization or Litigation? Time to Rethink the International Investment Regime', 8 July 2013.

'emergency health measures adopted in response to the COVID-19 pandemic...to come under attack by investors': see, for example, 'Could COVID-19 Emergency Measures Give Rise to Investment Claims? First Reflections from Italy', *Global Arbitration Review*, 26 March 2020. See also Michael Ostrove, Kate Brown de Vejar, and Ben Sanderson, 'COVID-19—A Legitimate Basis for Investment Claims?', *DLA Piper Alert*, 16 April 2020.

'"the US government made extensive use of threats of military action"': Srividya Jandhyala, Geoffrey Gertz, and Lauge N. S. Poulsen, 'Legalization and Diplomacy: American Power and the Investment Regime', paper delivered at the Department of Politics of Princeton University, 6 April 2016.

'In-house lawyers of large US companies...investment treaties': Jason W. Yackee, 'Do Bilateral Investment Treaties Promote Foreign Direct Investment? Some Hints from Alternative Evidence', *Virginia Journal of International Law* 51 (2011): 397.

Effects of France's BITs: Jason W. Yackee, 'Do BITs "Work"? Empirical Evidence from France', *Journal of International Dispute Settlement* 7 (2016): 55.

Arbitration

Studies on link between investment arbitration and investment flows globally and in other parts of the world are discussed in Jason W. Yackee, 'Do Bilateral Investment Treaties Promote Foreign Direct Investment? Some Hints from Alternative Evidence', *Virginia Journal of International Law* 51 (2011): 397.

'evidence linking foreign investments and economic growth': Maria Carkovic and Ross Levine, 'Does Foreign Direct Investment Accelerate Economic Growth?', in T. Moran, E. M. Graham, and M. Blomström (eds), *Does Foreign Direct Investment Promote Development?* (Institute for International Economics 2005).

'research...explores...investors accustomed to reliable institutions...look for the same thing abroad': Quintin Beazer and Daniel Blake, 'The Conditional Nature of Political Risk: How Home Institutions Influence the Location of Foreign Direct Investment', *American Journal of Political Science* 62 (2018): 470.

'in 2018 Japan had the world's largest investment outflow': *United Nations Conference on Trade and Development, Report on World Investment 2019*, figure 3, p. 4; in 2017 Japan ranked second; before that it was consistently among the top four.

'tobacco companies...have used the threat of investment arbitration': Jackie Calmes and Sabrina Tavernise, 'U.S. Proposes Provision on

Tobacco in Trade Pact', *The New York Times*, 2 October 2015 (threats against Namibia, Gabon, Togo, and Uganda).

'public policy in Canada...in investment arbitrations': Gus Van Harten and Dayna N. Scott, 'Investment Treaties and the Internal Vetting of Regulatory Proposals: A Case Study from Canada'. *Journal of International Dispute Settlement* 7 (2016): 92.

'diplomats...signing [BITs]...as a matter of workaday diplomacy...[and] to justify their salary and expensive international travels': Lauge N. S. Poulsen and Emma Aisbett, 'Diplomats Want Treaties: Diplomatic Agendas and Perks in the Investment Regime', *Journal of International Dispute Settlement* 7 (2016): 72.

'under what conditions may a state plead necessity (as many states have in emergencies, and as many more almost surely will in the wake of the COVID-19 pandemic)?': see Federica Paddeu and Freya Jephcott, 'COVID-19 and Defences in the Law of State Responsibility', Parts I and II, *EJIL: Talk!*, 17 March 2020.

'suspicion that investment arbitrators are business-biased': Thomas Schultz, 'Arbitral Decision-Making: Legal Realism and Law & Economics', *Journal of International Dispute Settlement* 6 (2015): 231.

'investors win in only 35–45 per cent of the cases': see the figures continuously reported by UNCTAD, Investment Policy Hub, Investment Dispute Settlement Navigator, https://investmentpolicy.unctad.org and the analysis (these statistics are more complicated than at first they might appear) in Thomas Schultz and Cédric Dupont, 'Investment Arbitration: Promoting the Rule of Law or Over-empowering Investors?' *European Journal of International Law*, 25 (2014): 1147, 1157–60.

'"egregious errors in the reasoning"': Federico Ortino, 'Legal Reasoning of International Investment Tribunals: A Typology of Egregious Failures', *Journal of International Dispute Settlement* 3 (2012): 31.

'By 2012, fifteen arbitrators had handled 55 per cent of all investment cases': Cecilia Olivet and Pia Eberhardt, *Profiting from Injustice: How Law Firms, Arbitrators and Financiers Are Fuelling an Investment Arbitration Boom* (Corporate Europe Observatory 2012), p. 38.

'"states...recalibrate[ing] their BITs"': Yoram Z. Haftel and Alexander Thompson, 'Legitimation through Renegotiation: Do

States Seek More Regulatory Space in their BITs?', submitted for publication as of mid-2020, also presented as conference paper at the University of Oslo, 2015.

'World Economic Forum in Davos...preserving "adequate policy space"': Karl P. Sauvant, 'The Evolving International Investment Law and Policy Regime: Ways Forward' (International Centre for Trade and Sustainable Development & World Economic Forum, Policy Options Paper 2016), p. 15.

'states...appreciate the risk of...investment arbitration only once it actually occurs': Lauge N. S. Poulsen and Emma Aisbett, 'When the Claim Hits: Bilateral Investment Treaties and Bounded Rational Learning' *World Politics*, 65 (2013): 273.

'a major book was published': Michael Waibel et al. (eds), *The Backlash Against Investment Arbitration. Perceptions and Reality* (Kluwer Law International 2010).

'More than half the investment claims ever filed': figures are continuously updated by UNCTAD, Investment Policy Hub, Investment Dispute Settlement Navigator, https://investmentpolicy.unctad.org

'"manning the barricades"': David Schneiderman, 'The Paranoid Style of Investment Lawyers and Arbitrators: Investment Law Norm Entrepreneurs and their Critics' in C. L. Lim (ed.), *Alternative Visions of the International Law on Foreign Investment* (Cambridge University Press 2016).

'In 2012 two whistle-blowers': Cecilia Olivet and Pia Eberhardt, *Profiting from Injustice: How Law Firms, Arbitrators and Financiers Are Fuelling an Investment Arbitration Boom* (Corporate Europe Observatory 2012).

Chapter 6: Where is arbitration going?

'"far-reaching power play orchestrated by...corporations"': Jessica Silver-Greenberg and Robert Gebeloff, 'Beware the Fine Print, Part I: Arbitration Everywhere, Stacking the Deck of Justice', *The New York Times*, 31 October 2015.

'"the implementation of this laudable idea has been disastrous"': Terra Lawson-Remer, 'Investor-State Dispute Settlement: The Arbitration Game', *The Economist*, 11 October 2014.

'Republican appointees': *Epic Systems Corp.* v. *Lewis et al*, 138 S.Ct. 1612 (Gorsuch, J. 2018; Thomas concurring; Ginsburg, J., dissenting joined by Breyer, Sotomayor, and Kagan).

Further reading

Chapter 1: What is arbitration and where does it come from?

John G. Collier and A. Vaughan Lowe, *The Settlement of Disputes in International Law: Institutions and Procedures* (Oxford University Press 1999).

Thomas Dietz, *Global Order Beyond Law: How Information and Communication Technologies Facilitate Relational Contracting in International Trade* (Hart 2014).

Christine Gray, 'Why States Resort to Litigation in Cases Concerning the Use of Force' in Nathalie Klein (ed.), *Litigating International Law Disputes: Weighing the Options* (Cambridge University Press 2014).

Christine Gray and Benedict Kingsbury, 'Developments in Dispute Settlement: Interstate Arbitration Since 1945', *British Yearbook of International Law* 63 (1992): 97.

Thomas Hale, *Between Interests and Law: The Politics of Transnational Commercial Disputes* (Cambridge University Press 2015).

Alain Pellet, 'The Case Law of the ICJ in Investment Arbitration', *ICSID Review* 28 (2013): 223.

Cesare P. R. Romano, 'A Taxonomy of International Rule of Law Institutions', *Journal of International Dispute Settlement* 2 (2011): 241.

Alec Stone Sweet, 'The New "Lex Mercatoria" and Transnational Governance', *Journal of European Public Policy* 13 (2006): 627.

Chapter 2: How arbitration works

Gary B. Born, *International Arbitration: Law and Practice* (2nd edn) (Wolters Kluwer 2016).

Matti S. Kurkela and Santu Turunen, Due Process in International Commercial Arbitration (2nd edn) (Oxford University Press 2010).

William W. Park, 'Equality of Arms in Arbitration: Cost and Benefits' in Mélanges en l'honneur de Pierre Mayer (L.G.D.J 2015), pp. 663–77.

Chapter 4: Arbitration and the law

The text of 'The New York Convention of 1958' ('The Convention on the Recognition and Enforcement of Foreign Arbitral Awards') is available at: http://www.newyorkconvention.org

Kathrin Betz, 'Proving Bribery' in *Fraud and Money Laundering in International Arbitration: On applicable Criminal Law and Evidence* (Cambridge University Press 2017).

Nigel Blackaby, Constantine Partasides, Alan Redfern, and Martin Hunter, *Redfern and Hunter on International Arbitration* (6th edn) (Oxford University Press 2015).

Chapter 5: The politics of arbitration against governments

Jonathan Bonnitcha, Lauge N. S. Poulsen, and Michael Waibel, *The Political Economy of the Investment Treaty Regime* (Oxford University Press 2017).

Cédric Dupont and Thomas Schultz (eds), Empirical Studies on Investment Disputes, special issue of Journal of International Dispute Settlement 1 (2016).

Index

For the benefit of digital users, indexed terms that span two pages (e.g., 52–53) may, on occasion, appear on only one of those pages.

Index

DIPLOMACY
A Very Short Introduction
Joseph M. Siracusa

Like making war, diplomacy has been around a very long time, at least since the Bronze Age. It was primitive by today's standards, there were few rules, but it was a recognizable form of diplomacy. Since then, diplomacy has evolved greatly, coming to mean different things, to different persons, at different times, ranging from the elegant to the inelegant. Whatever one's definition, few could doubt that the course and consequences of the major events of modern international diplomacy have shaped and changed the global world in which we live. Joseph M. Siracusa introduces the subject of diplomacy from a historical perspective, providing examples from significant historical phases and episodes to illustrate the art of diplomacy in action.

'Professor Siracusa provides a lively introduction to diplomacy through the perspective of history.'

Gerry Woodard, Senior Fellow in Political Science at the University of Melbourne and former Australasian Ambassador in Asia

www.oup.com/vsi

GEOPOLITICS
A Very Short Introduction
Klaus Dodds

In certain places such as Iraq or Lebanon, moving a few feet either side of a territorial boundary can be a matter of life or death, dramatically highlighting the connections between place and politics. For a country's location and size as well as its sovereignty and resources all affect how the people that live there understand and interact with the wider world. Using wide-ranging examples, from historical maps to James Bond films and the rhetoric of political leaders like Churchill and George W. Bush, this Very Short Introduction shows why, for a full understanding of contemporary global politics, it is not just smart - it is essential - to be geopolitical.

'Engrossing study of a complex topic.'

Mick Herron, Geographical.

INTERNATIONAL RELATIONS
A Very Short Introduction
Paul Wilkinson

Of undoubtable relevance today, in a post-9-11 world of growing political tension and unease, this *Very Short Introduction* covers the topics essential to an understanding of modern international relations. Paul Wilkinson explains the theories and the practice that underlies the subject, and investigates issues ranging from foreign policy, arms control, and terrorism, to the environment and world poverty. He examines the role of organizations such as the United Nations and the European Union, as well as the influence of ethnic and religious movements and terrorist groups which also play a role in shaping the way states and governments interact. This up-to-date book is required reading for those seeking a new perspective to help untangle and decipher international events.

www.oup.com/vsi

LAW
A Very Short Introduction
Raymond Wacks

Law underlies our society - it protects our rights, imposes duties on each of us, and establishes a framework for the conduct of almost every social, political, and economic activity. The punishment of crime, compensation of the injured, and the enforcement of contracts are merely some of the tasks of a modern legal system. It also strives to achieve justice, promote freedom, and protect our security. This *Very Short Introduction* provides a clear, jargon-free account of modern legal systems, explaining how the law works both in the Western tradition and around the world.

THE UNITED NATIONS
A Very Short Introduction
Jussi M. Hanhimäki

With this much-needed introduction to the UN, Jussi Hanhimäki engages the current debate over the organization's effectiveness as he provides a clear understanding of how it was originally conceived, how it has come to its present form, and how it must confront new challenges in a rapidly changing world. After a brief history of the United Nations and its predecessor, the League of Nations, the author examines the UN's successes and failures as a guardian of international peace and security, as a promoter of human rights, as a protector of international law, and as an engineer of socio-economic development.

www.oup.com/vsi